RUNNING WILD

Dispelling the Myths of the African Wild Dog

John McNutt and Lesley Boggs
Photography by Hélène Heldring and Dave Hamman

Smithsonian Institution Press
Washington, D.C.

Produced for Southern Book Publishers by
Neville Poulter Design and Tracey Hawthorne Editorial Services

Published in the United States of America by Smithsonian Institution Press
ISBN 1 56098 717 0

Library of Congress Catalog Number is available
First edition, first impression 1996

First published in South Africa by Southern Book Publishers,
PO Box 3103, Halfway House 1685, South Africa

Designer Neville Poulter
Editor Tracey Hawthorne
Maps Loretta Giani
Reproduction cmyk pre-press
Printing and binding SNP Printing Pte Ltd, Singapore

Acknowledgements

Four years of persistence and determination have enabled us to complete this personally rewarding project on Africa's most endangered large carnivore, the African wild dog, which stole our hearts and enriched our souls. Our goal was to draw the attention of the reader to the plight of the African wild dog and to change the negative images and misunderstanding that surround this fascinating animal. We hope that the photographs in this book have helped to accomplish this.

Achieving our goal would not have been possible without the support and assistance of many people. Firstly, we thank the Botswana Government and the Department of Wildlife and National Parks for the opportunity to work in their wildlife areas. We would especially like to thank Peter and Beverly Pickford and Lex Hes, who so generously imparted their photographic knowledge, experience and advice, and whose encouragement gave us confidence to persist. Our sincere thanks to Colin Bell of Wilderness Safaris, whose enthusiasm and motivation put us on the right track four years ago; to Dr John ('Tico') McNutt and Lesley Boggs, for creating a superb and informative text; and to Tim and June Liversedge, whose film projects gave us the opportunity to be in the right place at the right time and without whom we would never have compiled such an extensive wild dog portfolio. A very special thank-you to Alain and Illona Schram, whose dear friendship will always be enormously appreciated, and Hennie and Angela Rawlinson and Arddyn Moolman, for their generous hospitality and friendship. To all at Okavango Wilderness Safaris, in particular Alan Wolfromm, Chris Kruger and the Mombo Camp staff, and at Sefofane Air Charters, whose assistance in keeping us fed, watered, fuelled, nursed, mobile, in communication and sane helped us immeasurably: we are deeply grateful. Thanks, too, to the Glass family, Tessa Redman and Trevor Earl, who welcomed us into their homes during the design and editing stage. We wish to thank Neville Poulter and Tracey Hawthorne, and Basil van Rooyen and Louise Grantham at Southern Books, for believing in this project and creating such a beautiful book. Our appreciation goes to Lesley Hay of ABPL, and to Russel Friedman for his valuable advice and guidance.

Lastly, to our parents, family and dear friends whose love and support have made all the difference: we dedicate this book to you.

Hélène Heldring and Dave Hamman

The authors are grateful to the Office of the President of Botswana for permission to conduct research in Botswana, and to the Department of Wildlife and National Parks for access to Botswana's national parks and reserves. Dr Richard Faust and Dr Markus Borner of the Frankfurt Zoological Society were especially supportive of the field research project, and FZS – Help for Threatened Wildlife provided generous financial support (FZS project no. 1056/87). Rod Mast of Conservation International and Dr John Ledger of the Endangered Wildlife Trust gave encouragement and financial support instrumental in helping establish and maintain the field project, particularly in the initial few years.

Numerous local businesses provided services or funding to support our research in a multitude of ways. These included Air Botswana, the Booking Company, Gametrackers Botswana, Ker and Downey, Moremi Safaris, Ngami Data Services, Safari South, Shell Oil Botswana and Okavango Wilderness Safaris. The Zoological Society of Philadelphia, especially Bill Konstant, and Dave Wood deserve mention for their enthusiasm and commitment to support conservation research from Philadelphia. Rod Hall and British Airways, and Dave Gibson of USAfrica Airways, helped enormously through their commitment to assisting nature conservation by providing travel between Botswana and the United States.

Private donors – too many to list – contributed independently to the financial operations of the project. Their support for our research project was important not only because it helped keep the field operations running smoothly, but because it was given from the heart with the belief that our work in Botswana was important and in some way enduring. Especially among those who contributed privately were Lee Belcher, John Brittingham, Richard Buthe, Christian and Midori Fulghum, Chris Harvey, Shirley Metz, Louise Meiras, Ric Owens, Tom Richards and Neil Taylor.

The people of Maun generously and continuously opened their homes, shared their lives, their friends and families, and gave of themselves in ways that have made living and working in Botswana a deeply rewarding personal experience for us. Especially among those were Tim and Bryony Longden, Hennie and Angela Rawlinson, Adam and Brigitte Hedges, Paul and Diana Larkin, Peter Perlstein, Derek Flatt, Paul Sheller, Ron Crous, Mike Lorenz, Karen Ross, Salome Meyer and Peter Comley. There are too many to list them all by name and we apologise to those we have left out.

Many people assisted with field research over the years, and we especially acknowledge the help of Kenneth Molepo, research assistant and ambassador for the project in rural communities, and Boisenikitso Motshoiki, our camp manager. John Bulger shared his knowledge of wild dogs in the Okavango, and his suggestions proved invaluable in establishing a study site and initiating field research.

For advice, ideas and encouragement while writing the text for this book we are grateful to John Galaty and Peter Pickford. We are forever indebted to our families, who were enthusiastic and supportive throughout.

Finally, the dogs.

John McNutt and Lesley Boggs

Foreword

≈

Ever since we domesticated cattle, sheep and goats, we have been locked in battle with the carnivores that prey upon our livestock. The conflict around the globe has been similar, although the species may be different: Europeans against wolves and foxes, Americans against wolves and coyotes, Australians against dingoes, and Africans against a fearsome array of lions, leopards, hyenas, jackals . . . and wild dogs.

In all parts of the world the war against the carnivore has been won by man, and now only remnants of once widespread species remain. The African wild dog has been eliminated from most of its former range, and today there are only three populations left on the continent in the kind of numbers that might ensure their survival for the foreseeable future – and even these populations are highly vulnerable to genetic degradation and events such as epidemic diseases, which recently killed all the wild dogs of the Serengeti in Tanzania.

Africa faces formidable environmental problems as human numbers increase and conflicts with wild animals escalate. The race is on to save the endangered species of the continent, and the meagre weapons on the side of conservationists are knowledge, understanding and empathy for the wild cousins of the very animals we have chosen to be our companions in childhood, family life, old age and blindness.

This book is a major contribution to our perceptions about the African wild dog, and it deserves to be read by a wide variety of people, to broaden their knowledge and arouse their compassion.

Dr John Ledger
Director
Endangered Wildlife Trust

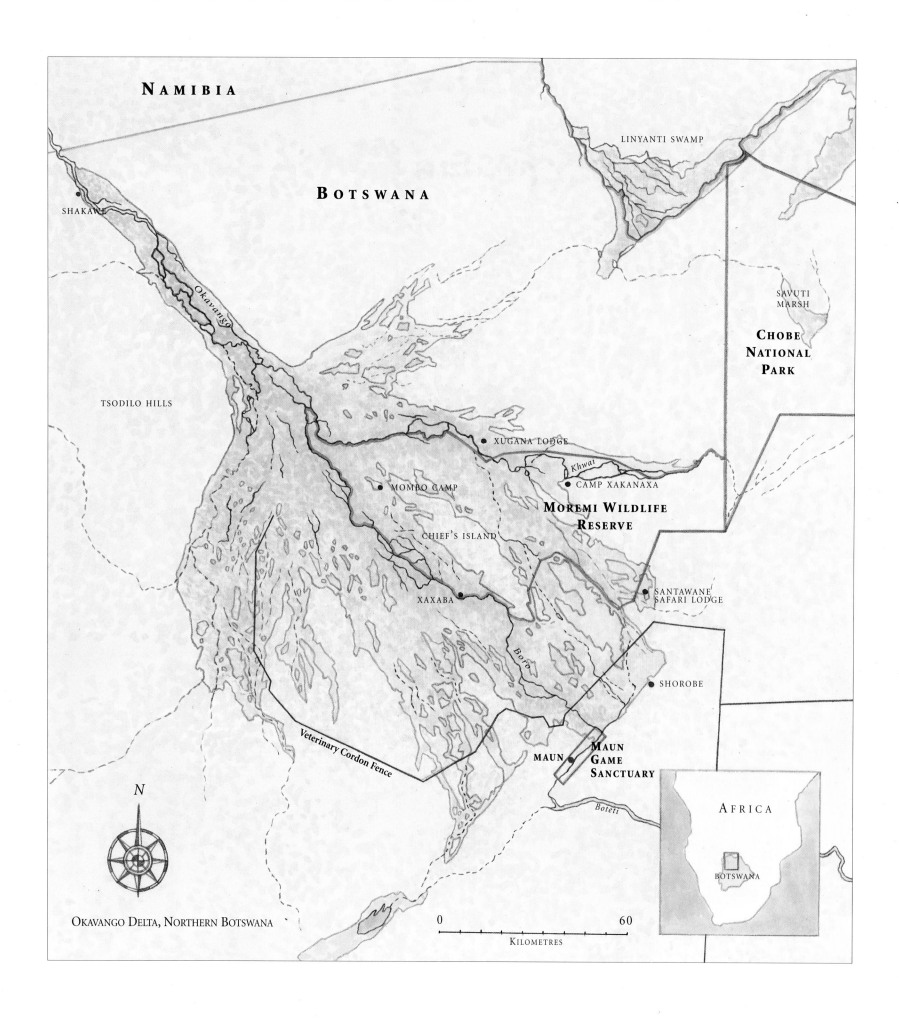

NAMIBIA

BOTSWANA

LINYANTI SWAMP

SHAKAWE

Okavango

SAVUTI
MARSH

CHOBE
NATIONAL
PARK

TSODILO HILLS

XUGANA LODGE

Khwai

MOMBO CAMP

CAMP XAKANAXA

MOREMI WILDLIFE
RESERVE

CHIEF'S ISLAND

SANTAWANE
SAFARI LODGE

XAXABA

Boro

SHOROBE

Veterinary Cordon Fence

MAUN
GAME
SANCTUARY

MAUN

Boteti

N

AFRICA

BOTSWANA

OKAVANGO DELTA, NORTHERN BOTSWANA

0

60

KILOMETRES

Contents

Prologue

"'What big teeth you have!" said Little Red Riding Hood.

"All the better to eat you with," said the wolf.'

Where in our perception of large canids does reality end

and myth take over to fill in what we actually do not know?

After weeks of hearing my friend and fellow wildlife biologist John Bulger describe how much luck was required to find wild dogs in northern Botswana, I still did not appreciate how difficult it would be. I knew he had spent many months pursuing reports and following tracks only to come away with the unsatisfying knowledge that the dogs had been there and were gone. Nonetheless, I maintained an unreasonable – probably disconcerting – blend of optimism and enthusiasm, born largely of ignorance of the magnitude of the challenge facing us.

The first time we set out together to reconnoitre the Moremi Wildlife Reserve in search of wild dogs, extremely good luck fuelled my enthusiasm. As the light began to fade on our first day out, we were beginning to think about setting up camp for the night. We had been bouncing around for more than five hours in our battered old Land Cruiser packed with camping equipment. John was explaining that he had twice seen a pack in the vicinity in the past year, when we rounded a bend in the sandy track and suddenly came upon that very pack of wild dogs, lying in the open beside the track.

Even I could appreciate the luck of our timing, and I had the almost mystical feeling that the pack had been waiting there for us. 'It's not usually like this,' John said repeatedly, presumably in an attempt to stem my soaring optimism about conducting field research to study the dogs' behaviour. In the dusk we were able to follow them only briefly as they ducked into the thick bush, waving their white tails, a kind of challenge for us to attempt following them into the as yet uncompromised Okavango.

Previous page, left. *Shoulder to shoulder, two subordinates initiate the greeting ritual to rally the pack.*

Previous page, right. *An inquisitive and alert pup epitomises the status of African wild dogs. Currently classified as 'Vulnerable', reclassification to 'Endangered' has been recommended.*

Above. *The familiar profile of a wild dog shows why it might be mistaken for a feral domestic dog but recent genetic analyses indicate that* Lycaon *diverged from its closest wolf-like relatives more than two million years ago.*

That was in July 1989. Six months later we had managed to locate only two additional packs of dogs. By the end of 1990, with considerable luck and the help of numerous tourist-safari operators, seven packs were included in the study, within an area of approximately 2 500 square kilometres; at that point, we felt reasonably confident that we knew most of, although probably not all, the dogs in the area. By the end of 1992 there were 12 packs of wild dogs included in the study within the same area, but to this day, after more than six years of field research, we cannot say with certainty that we know of all the dogs in the area. Our not seeing them does not mean they are not there, and our study area is simply too large and too infrequently visited to expect that all dogs would necessarily be seen.

The focus of our African wild dog research, which began in earnest a couple of months after our first introduction to the Mboma pack in the Moremi Wildlife Reserve, has been continuously to monitor a sample population of 80 to 150 free-ranging wild dogs, in order to identify behavioural and population characteristics for the wild dogs in northern Botswana. Because this is one of the last remaining, relatively large, unconstrained and unprotected wild dog populations on the planet, these characteristics are essential to evaluating the population's long-term prospects for survival in this part of the world.

African wild dogs (*Lycaon pictus*), previously known as Cape hunting dogs and, more recently and more appropriately, painted dogs, were once distributed widely throughout sub-Saharan Africa. Over the past 100 years their range has been reduced to relatively few small populations, mostly isolated in protected areas in east and southern Africa. The precipitous decline of wild dog numbers and range can be attributed to habitat loss and fragmentation and to expanding human and domestic-livestock populations which conflict with large carnivores of all species.

Until recently, wild dogs were systematically exterminated in predator-control efforts, in response to conflict primarily with livestock but also with wildlife 'buck' in reserves and national parks. *Lycaon* is classified as 'Vulnerable' by the World Conservation Union (IUCN) but, on the basis of recent surveys and an IUCN-sponsored *Lycaon* workshop in 1992, reclassification to 'Endangered' has been recommended. The total estimate for the wild dogs in the whole of Africa is fewer than 5 000 individuals, and only three populations estimated to contain more than 350 adults each are known to remain: one in Selous Game Reserve in Tanzania, one in the Kruger National Park in South Africa, and this population in northern Botswana.

Botswana is unusual among African countries by virtue of its extremely low human

Above. *Soft whining and twittering vocalisations accompany lowered ears and wagging tails in the submissive behaviours characteristic of the constant social contact between pack members.*

population density and the consequent under-development of natural areas. Although changing rapidly, this is particularly true of the Okavango Delta, which has experienced comparatively little human-related change since David Livingstone first drew attention to the region in 1857. In addition to its remoteness at the northeast fringe of the semi-arid Kalahari desert, early travellers to the Okavango were discouraged by the full com-plement of dangerous African wildlife and a per-sistent risk of diseases. These included malaria and sleeping sickness carried by the tsetse fly. Modern attempts to eradicate tsetse flies in the Okavango Delta have failed to date, and the region remains relatively undeveloped and free of domestic livestock. Ungulate populations in the Okavango and surrounding areas support healthy populations of all the African large carnivores, and the wild dog population of northern Botswana, associated primarily with this region,

Above. *A pack has usually travelled several kilometres before the first warm rays of morning dissolve the cool night away. Wild dogs tend to hunt early in the morning, before temperatures grow too hot.*

Top right. *Splashed with white 'paint', an older male, appearing weary, brings up the rear as the pack departs on the evening hunt.*
Above right. *Young pups actively explore their surroundings with their mouths. Whether it be a sibling's ear or dry 'buffalo chips', there is a vast amount to be learned about the world before they become contributing members of the pack.*

is the largest remaining unprotected African wild dog population on the continent.

The wild dog appears to have been inhabiting the African landscape as long as if not longer than humans. It is the largest wild canid in Africa and preys primarily on medium-sized ungulates. Recent genetic analyses, which have confirmed earlier classifications that placed *Lycaon* in a separate genus from the other wolf-like canids (a group that includes the grey wolf, *Canis lupus*, the coyote, *C. latrans*, and the African jackals, *C. mesomelas*, *C. adustus* and *C. aureus*), also suggest a divergence from the rest of these large canids around two to three million years ago. The first known fossils of *Lycaon* also support this date of divergence. *L. pictus* is the only living species in the genus *Lycaon*, and during its long and successful tenure in the African predator community it has evolved distinct morphological and physiological characteristics which

Above. *A pack led by several yearlings crosses a shallow flood plain while scanning the distance for potential prey.*
Left. *Back at the den, decorated with a dusting of dirt and grass stems from wrestling with litter mates, a pup rests while waiting for the returning adults. At the age of ten weeks pups already have developed a keen appetite for regurgitated meat.*
Opposite. *An adult male with a full belly responds lazily, with open mouth turned into a yawn, to a half-hearted request for a regurgitated snack.*

may make it uniquely adapted to sub-Saharan savanna and bushland habitats.

Wild dogs have always impressed natural historians with their efficiency as communal predators and their highly social behaviour. The organisation of wild dogs into packs, as is the case with many of the other canid species, has been functionally related to the capturing of large prey relative to their body size. There is little doubt that hunting in a group facilitates the successful capture of relatively large prey, but social organisation varies widely among canids and the causes underlying the extreme sociality reported for *Lycaon* may be more complex than a functional explanation of one of its consequences.

Our early scientific understanding of the behavioural ecology of *Lycaon* is limited to a set of records spanning several years in the Serengeti Plains ecosystem. Wild dogs are described as wolf-like, social carnivores which communally rear offspring in closely related kin groups. Wild dogs first made it into the behavioural-ecology headlines when they were described as unusual if not unique among social carnivores by virtue of their patrilineal (male-based) kin groups, from which females were said to emigrate. Among mammals, female emigration, male philopatry and patrilineal social organisation are uncommon characteristics. These were explained in the general context of a consistently reported sex-ratio bias in which males outnumber females by almost two to one.

However, most of these distinct and therefore more salient characteristics described in early reports of wild dog social behaviour have been called into question by our research in Botswana, which has shown that their natural history is not as accurately known as we believed. Most importantly, the variations we have observed in the basic life history of wild dogs emphasise the limits of our understanding of the overall behavioural ecology of this species.

Myth and Malevolence

Having reviewed the current literature about *Lycaon pictus* in books on the behaviour, ecology and evolution of the carnivores, we still find numerous tenacious and inaccurate myths about wild dogs in the general body of knowledge to which we loosely refer as 'natural history facts'.

Left. *A herd of buffalo grazes peacefully along the edges of a wooded island. Buffalo are one of the many species of ungulates in the Okavango that support healthy populations of large carnivores.*
Right. *A juvenile stares in bold curiosity at the camera. Tourists have only recently discovered the exciting experience of watching wild dogs in Botswana, and the dogs' near-total indifference to people has won the hearts of a large following.*

Most of these derive from a hodgepodge of early, usually inaccurate accounts of wild dogs by natural historians, which were likely to have been at least partially supplemented by accounts from local folklore.

> Wild dogs hunt in packs, killing wantonly far more than they need for food, and by methods of the utmost cruelty: *Lycaon* does not kill quickly as the lion does but often starts to devour the antelope which is his victim before life is extinct.
>
> They do more damage than almost any other carnivorae, for when they enter a particular stretch of country the disturbance they cause is so great that for the time being, all the buck are driven out: indeed, a strange absence of antelope from an area is often the first sign of the wild dogs' presence.
>
> A particularly unpleasant characteristic is that they will, without hesitation, turn upon any member of the pack that falls by the way through wound or sickness and show no reluctance to consume their own kind.
>
> *RM Beres, Director, Uganda National Parks, in Oryx 3: 180-182, 1956.*

Apart from the first five words, this piece of natural-history reporting – dating back only to 1956 – is nonsense and reflects a remarkable juxtaposition of wildly inaccurate myth and (following this description) an unusual and seemingly inconsistent management recommendation advocating the importance of wild dogs in maintaining healthy wildlife populations in national parks. It was as if the author himself struggled as a conscientious wildlife manager with the demons that have burdened some animals, and especially canids, with the unfortunate consequences of powerfully negative perceptions and attitudes derived not from facts but from our human values.

Although not a single sentence in the foregoing quote describing wild dogs is accurate (and note that nowhere does it suggest that the author has actually seen any of these characteristics), the paragraph is presented as fact and thereby contributes to further entrenching the various myths that abound in our collective understanding of these maligned animals.

These myths persist primarily because of the difficulty in acquiring detailed behavioural information about wild dogs in their natural habitat, but also, we believe, because of a widespread and deeply rooted predisposition among people

Above. *Buffalo are rarely of interest to wild dogs. As occasional hosts for important bovid diseases, however, buffalo are partially responsible for the persistence of a cattle-free Okavango still able to support wild dogs.*

Below. *Especially adapted to its marshy surroundings, a lechwe runs gracefully through its shallow, watery domain. The myth that wild*

dogs clear the bush of resident antelope ignores the fact that these antelope have co-evolved with wild dogs for millions of years.

Right. *Having successfully navigated a relatively wide, deep water channel, a wet pup is greeted by anxious adults. As hesitant pups delay crossing bodies of water, the anxiety of adults about the presence of crocodiles intensifies.*

almost everywhere in the world to vilify wild large canids. We are only now, late in the 20th century, beginning to understand and correct devastatingly negative perceptions of the natural versions of, ironically, 'man's best friend'.

The numerous myths about wild dogs that are perpetuated in accounts like the one quoted on the previous page are repeated over and again through time. When we hear snippets of this wild dog misinformation today, rather than simply dismiss the reports outright, we believe it is worthwhile to attempt to identify and explain their derivation. We assume that there is some

thread of reality, some aspect of the natural behaviour of wild dogs, that makes the beliefs seem credible. Therefore, we look for understanding in the highly variable empirical repertoire of their natural behaviour.

The myth of 'wanton killing of more than they can eat' is a particularly negative one from the perspective of ecosystem-management decisions. Surplus killing is an interesting phenomenon which has been recorded for numerous species of carnivores, from foxes in Europe to mountain lions in North America. In general, the characteristics of these recorded accounts show a

consistent pattern: they are usually found in circumstances where there is a superabundance of easy prey, such as cougars wreaking mayhem in a flock of sheep or lions falling on a herd of cattle with calves. Explanations to account for surplus killing include speculation about the training of inexperienced offspring and opportunistic prey capture by carnivores that cache food for later consumption. These accounts all have one thing in common, which is that the predator leaves an already secured prey to kill another.

We have never seen this behaviour in wild dogs. We suspect the myth can be explained by a

misinterpretation of an occurrence in which several of the pack members opportunistically chase different individuals from a herd of antelope. With numerous simultaneous chases occurring, it is not uncommon that more than one hunter succeeds in capturing prey. Occasionally more prey is caught than the pack of dogs can eat. This would undoubtedly be viewed as wasteful from a game manager's perspective. (Wild dog hunting behaviour is described in greater detail in Chapter Three.)

The myths about wild dogs' slow and cruel method of killing are remarkably entrenched in people's negative perception of them as vicious

killers. Few predators, and especially not lions, can be said to dispatch their prey faster or with more efficiency than wild dogs. These myths are clearly derived from anthropocentric judgments of what in nature is and is not cruel – clearly an inappropriate categorising of nature in order to fit our human cultural value systems. This subjective interpretation of nature is only now, in recent history, beginning to be understood, exposed and corrected in our perceptions of the natural world.

The myth of wild dogs cannibalising wounded or injured members of their species is particularly curious. Quite contrary to the myth, we have countless times seen wounded and badly injured wild dogs not only tolerated but cared for by members of the pack. We have never seen anything that would support the assertion that wild dogs will suddenly turn on their wounded and consume them. We suspect this myth derives, at least in part, from local folklore about wild dogs. From our investigations into local rural people's perceptions and knowledge of the natural history of wild dogs, we know of frightening stories that are entirely analogous with European children's stories about wolves such as *Little Red Riding Hood* and *The Three Little Pigs*. For example, a local Motswana who was raised in a rural area explained that they were always told as young children that wild dogs would kill and eat little children who strayed too far into the bush. It is possible that the myth of wild dog cannibalism is linked to a similar story intended to magnify the portrayal of dogs as vicious.

Folklore might be at the root of the general perpetuation of myths which categorise animals, or their behaviours, as 'good' or 'bad', but it is insufficient to explain the context of the myth itself. For that, we look for supporting evidence in the natural behaviour of wild dogs.

There are at least two naturally occurring contexts in which the behaviour of African wild dogs might be sufficiently misinterpreted to explain the origins and persistence of the cannibalism myth. It is true that wild dogs will fight, especially in territorial conflict between packs or over access to mates. It is also not uncommon for fights between packs to have fatal consequences for the losers, and we speculate that fatal fighting could have played a part in the origin of the cannibalism description.

Opposite top. *Yearling females return to the pack after an unsuccessful chase. The sheepish grin seems to say, 'Sorry, another miss.'*
Opposite bottom. *Lethargy sets in during a rest in the warm morning sun. Following a meal, the pack will eventually move into the shade, where it remains throughout the day. On exceptionally hot days, the dogs endure the sun to lie in pans of muddy water.*
Above. *A group of pups 'mobs' an adult to cajole him into regurgitating a meal from the morning hunt. Excitement caused by a returning hunter may be partly responsible for the myth that wild dogs will sometimes attack pack members.*

Secondly, the myth that wild dogs will attack other pack members that have blood on them, say from an injury – which we take to be a corollary of the 'aggressive cannibalism' myth – can be explained by something that commonly occurs when a pack is hunting. On some hunting forays a single adult might disappear into the bush on a chase while the rest of the pack gathers and quietly waits, sometimes for several minutes, for the hunter's return. If the hunter was successful in capturing prey, that dog returns from the kill with fresh blood matting its fur, especially on the head and neck. In the ensuing excitement, which is often expressed by a chorus of high-pitched twitters and vocalisations in greeting, the rest of the pack will mob the bloody hunter and hungry juveniles will whine obsequiously, begging the successful hunter

for a regurgitated taste. It seems probable that this 'mob scene', in the absence of a complete understanding of the events, could be interpreted as aggressive, particularly as the hunter often appears to be attempting to avoid the fray.

Myths or beliefs such as these that find their way into 'scientific literature', in the absence of strong contrary evidence, are like permanent scars on the character of the animals described. In the past, it seems the fundamental criterion for publishable natural-history material was not validity or reliability but rather consistency with existing beliefs. Once in print, the question of the veracity of the written account is removed by virtue of its publication, enabling if not obligating later reviewers and researchers to take it into account. When myths are character damaging,

Above. *A hungry subordinate leads the pack on the evening hunt. An average pack is successful about once in three hunting attempts.*
Opposite. *Unique natural markings of black, brown and white make every wild dog individually recognisable.*

especially those that are in some way consistent with components of human value systems, they become like chronic open wounds.

It is our hope, with the contents of this book, to dispel many if not most of these often damaging myths about African wild dogs in order to begin to heal the wounds while there is still time for reparation.

The Mombo Pack

Chief's Island, at approximately 40 kilometres in length, is the largest single dry-land area in the Okavango Delta. The photographs in these pages were taken over a four-year period at the northwest end of Chief's Island, at a special place called Mombo. In addition to a full complement

dogs but also the wild dog spirit for life in one of Africa's last great wilderness wetlands.

In the heart of the Okavango Delta the wild dogs of Mombo are insulated from the pressures of human and livestock activities which many of the wild dog packs living closer to the periphery of the delta experience. The Mombo pack represents for us what is possibly our closest living example of what most wild dog packs may have been like a hundred years ago.

From a demographic point of view, the Mombo pack may be considered uncharacteristic in several ways because of the specific geographic characteristics of their range at the top end of Chief's Island. With broad, nearly impenetrable, permanently flooded areas bordering them on the north and west, the Mombo pack is unusually buffered from contact with neighbours, where African wild dog packs elsewhere typically have neighbours overlapping their borders on all sides. This unusual geographical characteristic of the Mombo pack's range may begin to account for why, throughout our years of behavioural research on free-ranging wild dogs, they have consistently provided all the exceptions to the rules and defined the ranges of variation in the developing patterns of wild dog behaviour observed elsewhere in northern Botswana.

As if to prevent any presumptuous inclination of ours to say that wild dogs will behave in certain predictable ways, the Mombo pack always managed to do exactly what we thought wild dogs would not. For example, just when we believed we had a clear picture of the emigration behaviour of wild dogs, Mombo pack dogs did something completely contrary to what other packs have been doing for years; if we said we had never seen a pack of wild dogs kill buffalo or zebra, the Mombo pack would oblige, usually in front of several cameras; when we authoritatively asserted that wild dogs are frequently the focus of aggression by lions and always lose their kills to challenges by adult male lions, the Mombo pack chased not one but three adult males away, demonstrating that pack size and perhaps familiarity with residents occasionally can prevent loss of resources to aggressive lions.

The Mombo pack wild dogs have been our teachers, demonstrating with their persistently large pack membership and their concentrated

of the large carnivores of southern Africa, the Mombo area of Chief's Island supports unprecedented densities of medium-sized grazing animals. This is the playground of the Mombo pack of wild dogs.

The Mombo pack is the quintessential wild dog pack and the images that follow capture not only the subtle and fascinating behaviours of wild

activities in the Mombo area that, if given an appropriately healthy wilderness habitat in which to live, wild dogs can be surprisingly adaptable and will not easily be nailed down to simple descriptive characterisations.

The Mombo pack is well known by many tourists to the area, some of whom come to Mombo with the express purpose of spending some time with the wild dogs. The pack has been on the awkward end of countless camera lenses in the course of the last few years and recently has been the focus of numerous wildlife films. Their characteristic sufferance of the presence of people, with their noise, flashing cameras and exhausting vehicles, is remarkable and unparalleled in our experience with wildlife.

In fact, it is particularly this forgiving tolerance of humans that sets them so apart from the rest of the carnivores and so endears them to those of us who have had the good fortune to spend some of our time with them.

Pack

The mainstay of a wild dog pack is the union of the dominant male and female.

This essential partnership is struck virtually instantly,

with the first meeting of the wild dogs that form a new pack,

and usually persists unchanged for many years.

≈

A pack is defined in terms of its potential to reproduce and therefore must include at least one adult female and adult male. Occasionally a pack is as small as a single pair, but most are larger; even today, with most wild dog populations and their pack memberships declining precipitously, packs occasionally number as many as 40 to 50 dogs for short periods of time. Even in large packs the dogs that originally formed the pack, if not the dominant pair itself, remain constant as long as they survive. These individuals constitute for the pack the thread of continuity through time.

A wild dog pack should be thought of not as a static social unit but as a group with continuously changing membership. Throughout the year pack members of both sexes and various ages either leave the pack or die, and every successful year adds additional pups to the pack. Membership may not change for short periods (from day to day or week to week) but each year a pack's membership, with the exception of the initial breeding group that started the pack, differs considerably from the year before.

Packs persist for varying periods of time before eventually dying out. Some, but not all, packs leave behind descendants. Whether they succeed or fail depends on their success at reproduction and their survivorship. What constitutes a successful pack of wild dogs and why some are successful for many years while others fail and die out almost immediately are important research questions with complex answers. We can begin to answer them by looking at the various processes and determinants of a pack, starting at the beginning: the birth of a new pack.

The Birth of a New Pack

A pack is identified by its individual members (as opposed to a geographic area), and can be said to have a life cycle like that of any living organism: it has a beginning point, grows in relation to available resources and conditions and reproduces; its survival is affected by chance events and circumstances; and it eventually dies.

Dogs were calling last night around 03h00, behind the camp, in the direction of Kubu Pan.

06h15. Tracks of seven to eight dogs, on the road near the camp, to the old pole bridge. Which dogs?

09h30. Sighted from the plane, Lucky and Baron (both radio collars working) lying in a group of seven (yesterday there were five), about 3 km south of where the males were yesterday, toward Gomoti River.

10h50. On the ground, all four males (Tag, Bock, Baron and Lucky) are lying with three new, unknown females under an acacia; they have not eaten. Of the three new females, the yellow one is inserting herself between the other females and the males. Lucky is doing likewise with the males. New pack? There appears to be a pair already.

Journal notes, JWM, 25 January 1994.

A new pack begins when a female or several females from one pack join a male or several males from another. This event is actually a life-history process that has several antecedents. It usually begins with a single-sex group of wild dogs emigrating from its natal pack (the pack where they were born), like birds leaving a nest, to search for a lifetime of opportunity elsewhere.

For wild dogs, emigration from the natal pack takes one of two alternative routes, differen-

tiated by whether the individuals emigrating already have learned something from scent markings about the nearby presence of potential mates. The familiar behaviour of domestic dogs investigating and urinating on or near the faeces and urine, called scent marks, of other dogs in the neighbourhood is essentially identical to wild dog behaviour. Domestic dogs do not urinate randomly on car tyres; they do so because somewhere in the car's travels another dog has used the tyres as a scent-marking post. Once used in this way, the vehicle becomes a mobile chemical chain letter, moving from territory to territory and compelling resident dogs to respond. When a dog investigates those scent marks, some information is conveyed to the receiving dog.

Communication through scent marks might include information about sex (particularly whether only one sex is present in the group), and perhaps even the number of individuals. Wild dogs behave similarly when investigating marks

left by other wild dogs, and the mechanism of emigration from 'home' depends on whether or not information is already available through these marks about the presence of potential mates.

If the emigrating African wild dogs have no information about potential mates – a situation more often true for males – they simply leave their natal pack and begin moving through the ranges of other packs. Sometimes they travel impressive distances – over 200 kilometres has been recorded – presumably investigating whatever information is available to them about the presence of potential mates. By the same means, they frequently leave information about themselves.

The other mode of emigration initiates at the receiving end of marking communication. If a pack of dogs includes some young adult females old enough to leave and start their own pack, marks left by a group of itinerant males become of keen interest. By investigating these marks, residents gain information about the presence of

Previous page, left. *With an enduring gait, a wild dog pack trots into the setting sun.*
Previous page, right. *Energetic and full of mischief, two pups cavort in the soft sand excavated from the entrance to the den.*
Opposite, above. *An obliging mother patiently suckles a collection of young pups of varying sizes. Size differences of the pups indicate a pooled litter – not uncommon in large packs.*
Opposite, below. *Two adults tenderly lick the exposed underbelly of a younger sibling. Enthusiasm for pups by adult siblings and non-breeding subordinates is extreme when pups first start to venture out of the den but wanes as the pups grow.*
Above. *An aunt 'encourages' a young pup out of the safety of the den. Wild dogs use holes previously dug by antbears, spotted hyenas and warthogs.*

Above. *Although the pup is not hers, an adult female helper is very attentive to responding to its needs. In most packs only the dominant male and female mate and successfully reproduce, but their reproductive success is greatly increased with the cooperation of non-breeding helpers.*

Left. *Uncertain and uncoordinated, two pups emerge for the first time from the safety of the den, to view their expansive surroundings.*

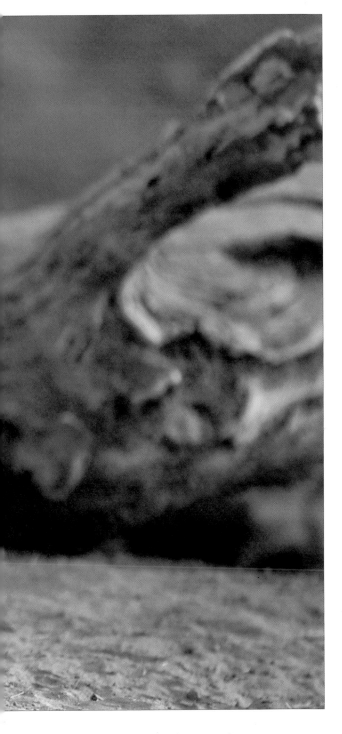

Above right. *Weaned at an early age, a pup stimulates an adult to regurgitate meat by licking and biting at its mouth. By regurgitating meat, all the adults in the pack are able to help feed the pups, illustrating the cooperative parental care that epitomises wild dog social behaviour.*

new dogs that may be potential mates for young adult females. Once aware of the presence of unknown males in the area, a young female may simply separate from the family group to search for them. Usually she will leave with at least one sister. It may take only a day or two for the males and females to locate each other, a remarkable event in itself in such vast areas.

Many times we have seen dogs from our study establish alliances with new, previously unknown dogs of the opposite sex. These groups always have managed to get together with new dogs within just a few days of leaving their natal pack. When we first see a new group we have no way of knowing if the new pack is only a few hours or a few days old. However, the excitement of being with new dogs is obvious as females devote their attention to their new male partners by behaving in ways which occur in no other context: they rub against the males and lift them by walking and squirming between their legs.

Very soon if not immediately after the formation of a new pack, the dominant male and female establish themselves in their respective social positions. In the presence of their new mate, the dominant male and female actively and aggressively establish or reinforce dominance

relationships, which may have been intact since they were small pups, with their siblings.

Dominant-subordinate relationships among litter mates are seldom obvious to an observer prior to the dogs' independence from the natal pack. This is primarily because wild dog packs are structured and function on the basis of age class, not on individual status. Dominance by one individual over a litter mate is seldom observed until after emigration, and fights between potential rivals for dominance are very infrequent. We have recorded only one such fight in seven years of field observations. This was a fight between two of four litter-mate sisters who were just over one year old at the time, but about five months before they would be expected to emigrate. They were participating at the time in the normal pack activity of helping their parents to care for the new litter of pups.

11h40. A fight about 250 m north of the den, just off the track to the water crossing. Yearlings. All four females were scuffling, very intent, in a cloud of dust. Difficult to see. In the middle, Delia and Ella lunged to gain a hold, biting and holding on, while Lana, Julia and, especially, Isaac lunged

repeatedly at the two as if intent on breaking up the fight. Isaac twittered repeatedly.

After about 70 seconds, Ella, very bloody about the head and neck, ran about 70 m away and lay at the edge of a termite mound and licked her wounds, whining. Julia, with her, also licked the wounds. Lana, Delia and Isaac returned to the den site and lay down near Alfred.

Journal notes, JWM, 24 July 1991.

After that fight we saw no sign of further aggression and the harmony and cooperation of the pack resumed. A week later there were not even visible scars on the loser. If we had not seen that fight, an event lasting only a few seconds, we might have no other evidence that such fights occasionally take place among siblings while they are still in their natal pack.

All four females emigrated five months later. Following the fight, the two 'losing side' sisters – the loser and the sister that had tended to her wounds – left the natal pack together and ultimately headed southeast, while the other two sisters dispersed in another direction. The first two sisters established a new pack about 20 kilometres from where they were born. The other two dogs may have been successful heading to

Above left. *Warming themselves in the early-morning sun, two well-fed pups struggle to stay awake. Pups from different litters differ in age by only a couple of weeks. Size differences obvious while pups are small become indistinguishable as they grow older.*

Above right. *With seemingly boundless energy, a group of pups gangs up on an adult. The pups' persistent begging, verging on harassment, elicits regurgitation by adults who have food to offer.*

the northwest and deeper into the Okavango swamps, but they were never seen again.

It is interesting that the two groups of sisters, several months after the fight, dispersed separately. The fight may have been a consequence of two of the sisters' inability to settle their relationship without fighting, despite the fact that a dominance relationship in wild dogs may not be expressed in any significant way or even be associated with any benefits until much later in life. However, from the start of a new pack and thereafter, dominance relationships become important. They also become reasonably unambiguous and are seldom contested. Among the numerous new

'pairs' that we have seen within a few days of their first meeting, we have observed no serious fights among the siblings. It seems likely that individual relationships are well established before potential mates enter the picture.

When a new pack has formed, it must establish a home range for itself in an area where it will not be threatened by challenges from other, resident wild dog packs. The dogs need to identify and begin to occupy an area that is not considered by another pack to be part of its core area. Home-range establishment begins immediately, as the dogs travel and urine mark to communicate their presence. In the case

Left. *Just less than three months old, this young pup already has the species' characteristic large ears and tricoloured coat. Pups are born black, with the white markings already clearly painted; the brown becomes noticeable only at about two months of age.*

Below. *Too anxious to wait for pups to come out, yearlings whine into the den entrance to wake up their siblings.*

Opposite, above. *A pup interrupts a private moment with its mother to ensure it is not missing any important activities with its litter mates.*

Opposite, below. *Having hastily eaten during a successful morning hunt, a yearling regurgitates for a sibling who remained at the den to baby-sit the pups. The baby-sitter, often a male, is usually a yearling, and full sibling to the pups.*

Mating and Reproduction

where males were itinerant before locating the females, the new pack usually starts to stake out a range at the edge of the female's natal pack. This 'budding off' on a piece of the female's natal home range may have several important functions: it should minimise conflict with neighbours because a parent pack may concede space to its daughters; and it allows the new pack to take advantage of the female's prior knowledge of the area, for example, where water can be found during the dry season.

Furthermore, several times we have seen females return to their natal pack after a new alliance with unknown males did not succeed for some reason – being close to home also can provide an opportunity for mate choice and a buffer against failed attempts at independence.

Once the home range is established and seems secure, a new pack of wild dogs wastes no time in making clear which of the adults is the dominant pair. By the time the mating season comes round, in March each year in Botswana, most of the wild dog packs have finalised the issue of who is going to mate. At this point the benefits associated with being dominant become clear, and subordinate adults that question the arrangements commonly are on the receiving end of short-tempered aggression from dominants intent on leaving no doubt about their status. This increase in aggressive dominance behaviour is part of a system which ultimately results in an extreme skew, or bias, in the reproductive success

Left. *Constant social contact, such as this casual, open-mouthed greeting between two members of the pack, occurs frequently as they lazily shift positions into and out of the sun through the heat of the day.*
Above. *The dominant female enjoys a quiet moment away from her pups. Constantly aware of their vulnerability, she keeps a weary but wary eye out for any potential danger.*

of the dominants compared to the other adult pack members. In most packs only the dominant male and female mate and successfully reproduce. Extremely skewed reproduction is unusual among other African social carnivores. Lions, for example, are quite egalitarian regarding who mates with whom, and hyenas are only slightly more structured in their social and reproductive behaviour, with several females mating but mainly with dominant males. The extreme skew in wild dog reproduction is matched only by some of the small social carnivores such as the dwarf mongoose, whose systems of social organisation and reproduction are nearly identical to those of African wild dogs.

The mechanism by which dominant dogs prevent other adults from mating appears to be primarily behavioural. A dominant male prevents subordinate males from mating with the oestrous dominant female by staying very close to her and not permitting any other male near, a behaviour called 'consorting'.

It is less clear how, or if, a dominant female actually suppresses the mating behaviour and oestrous cycling of subordinate females. In many packs more than one female will come into oestrus and mate. Subordinate females commonly come on heat several weeks after the dominant female. However, the outcome of the majority of these secondary pregnancies is the loss of the entire litter, probably in some way caused by the disposition of the dominant female. In most cases what happens to the lost pups is unknown because it takes place underground – dominant females have been observed absconding with a subordinate female's pups, taking them into her

own den; these youngsters seldom resurface. We have observed a few packs in which a subordinate female was allowed to keep some pups. These might be raised with the other, usually older, pups or, if the subordinate mother manages to prevent intervention by the dominant female, kept apart from the other pups by the subordinate mother until they are strong enough to clamber around above ground with their older cousins.

We frequently have seen pooled litters with pups of multiple sizes in Botswana. These are consistently found in large packs (consisting of more than 14 adults) and can easily be distinguished only while the pups are very young, when a difference in age of a few weeks is noticeable. The occurrence of multiple litters in a pack appears to be related to the size of the parent pack. Large packs are more likely to have multiple litters, as if the dominant female's ability to suppress or affect the reproductive activity of subordinates declines as the number of dogs in the pack increases. An alternative explanation is that the more adult dogs there are in a pack, the greater is the potential for feeding pups without disadvantaging the dominant female's litter. In this case, the dominant female would not be concerned about limiting the pack to her pups only, and would be disposed to allow her sisters to have pups as well.

Cooperative parental care for wild dog pups is one of the most fascinating aspects of the natural behaviour of wild dogs. At most, only a fraction of the adults in a pack reproduce during a single annual season. The others forgo their own direct reproduction and cooperate to care for the dominant pair's pups.

The most important characteristic of the average newly formed social group is that all the females are related to each other, as are all the males, because the two sub-groups that join to form a new pack are usually groups of full siblings. From a genetic perspective, although non-breeders do not have their own offspring to care for, those they provision and protect are close relatives (usually nieces and nephews).

Genetic relatedness is the fundamental link necessary to understand, from an evolutionary perspective, the consistent pattern of extremely skewed reproduction in wild dogs and the pattern of cooperative parental care by non-breeding adults. Quantitatively, all offspring produced by

Opposite. *Tongue-curling in submission to avoid a reprimand, a subordinate responds to the intent approach of the dominant female.*

Above. *Taking courage in small groups, helpers approach the den to visit the pups with heads lowered and ears lying flat. Exaggerated submissive posturing appears to minimise any misinterpretation of their intentions.*

Right. *The ability to accommodate unusually large litters – which average ten pups and occasionally number as many as 19 – is illustrated by this subordinate female whose teats are drying unused after she lost her pups to the dominant female.*

Left. *Sometimes pups accompany the pack to nearby water for a drink, before being encouraged to return to the den, with either the mother or a baby-sitter. Some adults head out impatiently while others hesitate, concerned for the pups.* **Below.** *Something in the distance attracts the focused attention of two yearlings. Sisters frequently form close friendships that may be related to the tendency to emigrate together, usually before the age of two years, in search of potential mates.*

sexually reproducing organisms have exactly half of their mother's genes and half of their father's. Offspring from the same parents, although not genetically identical (unless they come from a single zygote, as is the case, for example, with identical twins), share, on average, half of their genes with each of their full siblings. Given that each adult wild dog in a new pack is a sibling to one or the other of the breeding pair, the offspring of that pair will be genetically equivalent to exactly half the genetic value of any of the siblings of the dominant pair. In a genetic sense, then, a subordinate wild dog helping to care for and

protect a sister's or brother's pups is equivalent to that subordinate raising half that number of its own pups.

The cost of a subordinate wild dog's forgoing its own breeding may seem large in terms of reproductive success only until the options are considered. If the only option for a wild dog were to independently find a mate and reproduce elsewhere, the risk of complete failure because of the absence of helpers may be high. Taking this option might also jeopardise the success of the brother or sister for the same reason: too few helpers. If an individual's survival is enhanced by being in a group and reproductive success increases with the presence of helpers, then being a subordinate (even if non-breeding) adult in an average pack is a sensible adaptive option: it is far better to live in a pack as a subordinate and have some reproductive success, not to mention survive another year, than to risk an attempt to be independent with inadequate social support. Under these conditions, staying to help a sibling reproduce is a viable life-history decision.

In Botswana we have often seen pairs attempt to establish themselves as a pack and raise pups without helpers. Although we know of one pair that successfully raised three pups to one year,

most small packs fail with the death of one or both of the adults before any pups reach an age where they can participate in collective pack chores such as hunting, defence or chasing off competitors. Greater success associated with living in a group appears to be the mechanism favouring social cooperation and helping in dogs.

Hunting

There are various ways in which non-breeding adults contribute importantly to the success of a pack. Subordinate adults are often the most experienced and successful hunters. They routinely initiate the chases and may often make a kill by themselves before returning to collect the rest of the pack. Their hunting experience and skills are extremely important to the success of a pack because their participation reduces reliance on the breeding pair and reduces for all individual pack members the risks of incurring the potentially high costs, such as injury, associated with hunting large prey (see Chapter Three).

An African wild dog pack nearly always moves as a group through its home range and individuals, sometimes independently, sometimes

Above. *Stopping to gather at the edge of a small water channel before crossing, the pack appears unhurried and relaxed.*
Right. *While on the move, pack members continually stop to investigate marks left by neighbouring packs, then leave their own distinctive scent-mark signatures. Curious juveniles lag behind to investigate the marks left by their own pack.*

as a group, opportunistically chase prey animals as they are encountered.

A typical daily activity schedule is remarkably consistent for all packs of wild dogs in all populations. It consists of two active periods each day. At first light of dawn and last light of dusk, the pack routinely gathers, greets and starts off through its home range in search of prey. When it chases prey, usually medium-sized antelope, it typically does so as a group. If a large pack has more experienced hunters than a small pack, then the probability of the large pack's success at capturing prey should be greater, and its effort spent hunting less, than a small pack in the same circumstances.

Below. *Important tools that wear with age, a wild dog's teeth are adapted for tearing and cutting flesh. In good condition and put to effective use, these tools can dispatch a carcass with lightning speed.*

Bottom. *With bellies full to the point of bursting, a group of pups enjoys its first impala fresh rather than regurgitated.*

These may be important benefits to living in a large social group. Once a kill is made, sharing it with a limited number of additional pack members does not represent a loss for the dog or dogs that made the kill because wild dogs typically hunt relatively large animals, much larger than can be consumed by a single dog.

Another important benefit of social hunting is related to the fact that African wild dogs share their habitat with several other species which may be large and dangerous competitors; dogs always risk losing a kill to competitors if it is not eaten immediately. Being in a large group has several benefits in this regard. Firstly, having more individuals looking out for ambushing predators decreases the chances of the dogs' being taken by surprise; secondly, the more members in a group, the more resistance they can provide against

Opposite, above. *Standing head to tail, the dominant male and female flirt with each other for a moment. Bonds between successful mating pairs are strong and commonly endure for several years, ending only when one of the pair dies.*
Left. *The distinctive wild dog white tail tip shows up like a flag as they traverse the open flood plains. At a trot they seem to move effortlessly, and can travel in this gait for hours without a stop if the weather remains cool.*
Below. *Waking up from a long afternoon nap, a yearling gracefully arches her back and stretches before the social greeting that precedes the hunt.*

competitors; and lastly, the more mouths there are, the faster a kill can be eaten or carried away. It is not surprising to observe that an entire pack of wild dogs eating at a kill is organised, cooperative, fast, efficient and quiet, and that once finished it leaves and does not return.

During most of the year the pack ranges broadly in its vast home range, always pushing at the boundaries with its neighbours and leaving information about its presence in the form of urine and faecal marks. A wild dog pack's home range is not a 'territory' per se, because it has 'soft' boundaries with neighbours, meaning there is considerable overlap of a pack's range with the ranges of its various neighbours. Neighbouring packs seldom encounter each other, but when they do, depending on the kin relationships between the packs, these encounters may be aggressive and may include fighting. The few times we have seen two packs meet, the smaller pack was always chased away by the larger, but there was never an indication of a specific area boundary related to the chase or to the direction or distance of retreat of the 'losing' pack. It seems that the threat of a physical clash between packs is sufficient to maintain area boundaries between neighbours.

Above. *A pack takes refuge from the sweltering midday heat in the only shade in the vicinity. Temperatures commonly reach 40 degrees in the summer in northern Botswana and wild dogs endure it in a state of inactive discomfort, conserving their energy for the evening hunt.*
Left. *Packs that live in the heart of the Okavango Delta are accustomed to crossing relatively shallow flooded areas, and will take advantage of the opportunity to cool off when the temperatures soar. Shallow water is considered safe enough to play in, and even the older dogs occasionally partake in a wet romp.*
Opposite. *The common misconception that wild dogs are feral – domestic dogs gone wild – is an unfortunate consequence of their name and their familiar appearance.*

In the Okavango Delta home ranges average about 400 to 450 square kilometres. Elsewhere, in habitats supporting lower densities of prey animals, such as the dry central region of Botswana, wild dog home ranges can be several times larger than the average for packs in the relatively rich riparian areas of the Okavango Delta, and the Cuando and Linyanti rivers.

Even in dense areas with relatively small home ranges, wild dogs travel huge distances every day, a ranging behaviour which has been described as nomadic. 'Nomadism', implying no pattern of movement, does not precisely describe wild dogs because the ranging behaviour of wild dog packs clearly identifies boundaries that remain relatively constant through time. A pack travels through its range, stopping only at soft boundaries to mark, leaving fresh messages about its presence for neighbouring packs and probably, in the same sense, gathering information about those neighbours at the same time.

Cooperation

The pack's wide-ranging behaviour changes radically during the period of the year when pups are born and are too small to move with the pack. During the weeks prior to this time the pack will have investigated numerous potential den sites, with the dominant female especially keen to investigate and dig out abandoned dens that may have been used previously by antbears, hyenas, warthogs, snakes and even leopards; what criteria she uses to decide which site is the right one is anybody's guess. Occasionally a pack will return to a den in which it raised pups before, but more often it uses a different den each year. Approximately ten weeks after the dominant pair has mated, the heavily pregnant female goes underground and does not come up until a day or two later, after her pups are born. Once she has whelped her pups, the daily routine of the pack changes from ranging throughout its huge home range to round-trip forays from the den within a much smaller area, usually less than 100 square kilometres.

While caring for pups at the den, typically during the cooler months of June, July and August in northern Botswana, the cooperative nature of wild dogs becomes most pronounced. While the mother of the pups remains under-

ground in the den, the remainder of the pack leaves to go hunting, still on its daily dawn and dusk schedule. When a kill is made it is consumed quickly by all the dogs in the hunting party, after which they return directly to the den.

At the den several pack members, including subordinates, feed the mother of the pups by regurgitating meat in response to her begging whines. In this way each individual member of the pack is important, as a conveyor of food from the distant kill to the stationary reproductive centre of the pack.

As the pups grow older, the help of non-breeding adults becomes even more valuable. At only four weeks of age the pups start to poke their heads out of the entrance to the den, and when they do they are met with excited adults they have never seen before. Curiously, these adults seem to be beside themselves with the opportunity to regurgitate meat to the pups, which the pups waste no time in wolfing down. Over time, the excitement and enthusiasm of the helpers for the new pups wear off as their voracious appetites grow faster than the pups themselves.

Right. *Although wild dogs in East Africa often prey upon wildebeest, they rarely do so in Botswana. However, being opportunistic hunters, they never miss the chance to size up a herd.*
Below. *Bounding through the deeper water crossings, a group wastes no time in getting to the other side. With the threat of crocodiles, crossing deep channels can have fatal consequences.*
Opposite. *Each individual wild dog has uniquely 'painted' markings in brown, black and white. These tricoloured coats provide markings that conveniently enable researchers to identify all individuals in a population.*

As time passes the mother grows increasingly anxious to join the pack hunting, probably to increase her intake of food and fluids, but possibly just to have a break from the pups and the den site. When the mother leaves with the rest of the pack to go hunting, she nearly always leaves an adult, sometimes called a 'baby-sitter', at the den with the pups. This might be an older subordinate adult, possibly one that is injured, but is more commonly a yearling, and usually a full sibling to the pups in the den. The responsibility of the baby-sitter appears to be to ensure that the pups remain down the hole should a predator such as a lion approach.

The availability of a willing baby-sitter identifies an important difference between a newly formed pack, which has among its members only adult siblings of one or the other of the breeding pair, and an established pack, which has successfully raised young in previous years. New packs, which are usually smaller in their first year than in subsequent years, more frequently leave pups unattended while out hunting, while packs that have offspring from previous years very rarely do. Hence, subordinate adults in a new pack appear less likely to undertake or to be entrusted with the baby-sitting job than full siblings of the pups.

This may be a decision by the dominant female, who is less likely to leave her pups in the care of a subordinate adult (which could be viewed as a potential competitor for a breeding opportunity) than she would one of her own offspring (which has no potential conflict).

As the wild dog pups grow ever more active, exploring farther from the den, they become difficult to manage. At the age of 12 weeks they are less frightened by the world outside the den and more insistent about following the adults around, even when the adults are trying to leave to go hunting. Tactics used by adults to ensure that pups do not follow them become comical as their effectiveness decreases. Adults commonly resort to sneaking away quietly, or growling an alarm to frighten pups back into the den before quietly leaving on a hunt. Eventually, by the time the pups reach the age of three or four months, no tactics are sufficient to convince or coerce the pups to remain behind at the den.

At first, pups following the adults from the den tire quickly and are hidden or left behind at some point in the hunt and then collected later. As they grow stronger they become better at keeping up and are sometimes, even at as young as five months, right on the heels of adults in open-terrain chases which allow them to follow the hunt visually.

Once the pups have left the den the real school of life – experience – begins for them. There is much to be learned about hunting and avoiding dangerous predators for young wild dogs, and the education process is long. Distractions are always popping up, and some pups seem much more interested in investigating new things like vultures and francolins, or flowers and insects, than focusing on the important lessons of life. The price of inattention can be

high: pups being typical pups, playing or wandering off, sometimes pay with their lives. Mortality among pups of up to one year of age, mostly from lions, averages more than 60 per cent in northern Botswana. Even for the most serious young dogs, skills develop slowly and most do not begin participating effectively in prey capture with the rest of the pack until they are almost a year old. By this time, mating has already occurred among the adults and the dominant female is heavily pregnant again.

The pack's first year is often the most difficult and can determine its long-term fate. Some packs fail to become established, either as a consequence of natural mortality or as a result of conflict with other dogs. Some die out entirely as a group in the first year. Particularly damaging

to a pack is the loss of an entire litter of pups, from predation either directly on the pups or on the mother while the pups are still young. Wholesale loss of the pups for the year or loss of the breeding adults in a pack can weaken the pack sufficiently that it becomes susceptible to challenges by other dogs competing for territory, or that it forces the remaining dogs to leave in search of new mates.

On the other hand, success tends to breed success – a positive-feedback system where helpers contribute to produce more helpers for the following year. The presence of yearlings at the den site is a sign of success, indicating that the pack managed to get some of the previous year's litter through the narrow window of survival to adulthood. In northern Botswana we know of

four packs in which the same dominant pair produced a litter of pups each year for five consecutive years. During this time the various packs grew from as few as five adults to as many as 28 dogs, including pups.

As a pack grows with successive and successful (in terms of below-average mortality) litters of pups, the group can grow to be excessively large. While a large pack can have several benefits, for example, in terms of increased survival, a large group also may have negative consequences for some members. For each additional dog there is less food per kill, and the contribution of each

helper diminishes with each additional individual. Above a certain size, in fact, additional dogs may add no effective help at all.

At this point young adult wild dogs – those between the ages of one and three years – may opt to leave their natal pack, find their own mates, establish a new pack and attempt to reproduce independently, in the manner described at the beginning of this chapter.

In this way – having produced pups, some of which survive to adulthood, and some of which eventually emigrate to successfully start their own, new packs – a pack comes full circle.

Opposite, above. *While several dogs are engaged in hastily feeding from an impala carcass, other pack members keep an alert look-out for predators that might aspire to steal their kill.*
Opposite, below. *Tears in the soft ears of wild dogs occur frequently during high-speed chases through thick acacia scrub. These 'notches' are another distinctive characteristic that facilitates individual recognition.*
Above. *Wild dogs suffer from an undeserved reputation for being malevolent and vicious killers.*

Play

The light-hearted playfulness of wild dog pups belies the potential importance of play

and its social consequences. At a very young age litter mates engage in social play that

coincides not only with developing motor skills but also with the beginning of important

social relationships that will endure, in some cases, for the rest of their lives.

Few concepts in the study of animal behaviour present more of a quandary to scientists than play. Play is predominantly a characteristic of young, developing animals and is a category of behaviour that is widely recognisable even by those who know little else about animals. At the same time, it defies unambiguous definition. The most accepted definition of play centres most, in fact, on what it is not; play is defined as 'activity which appears to have no immediate benefits for the player'.

Although the defining characteristic of play is that it appears to have no immediate purpose, its assumed function is developmental, its putative benefits to be reaped at some time in the future. In this sense, perhaps the most significant consequence of play between wild dogs, with litter mates, in its forms of chasing, tackling and wrestling, is its effect on the process of learning the consequences of aggressive interactions.

The primary reason play behaviour represents such a puzzle to behavioural science is that while there appear to be no immediate benefits, costs such as energy expended, risk of injury and risk of attracting predators seem self-evident and have the potential to be life threatening. If play bears any costs, then some benefits must be derived from it to account for its nearly universal existence among social mammals. Because play is especially common among social mammals, we assume it has some beneficial role in the development of important traits related to social behaviour, such as group cohesion, but demonstrating this relationship has proven to be troublesome.

Previous page, left. *Unable to contain their excitement, several adults vie for the attention of a small pup outside the entrance to the den.*
Previous page, right. *Latching on to a sibling's tail, pups engage in a bodily tug-of-war. Some individuals are more aggressive than others by nature, and direct much of their attention to initiating play with litter mates.*
Above. *A leopard tortoise presents a perplexed youngster with a novelty.*
Left. *Objects commonly found around the den take on added significance if they can be used in some form of social play. Here, two pups dispute possession of a piece of grass.*

The costs of play, on the other hand, are more immediately discernible. We frequently have observed small pups with injuries that almost certainly occurred while they were playing. For example, it is common to see a small pup limping with an apparent leg injury. Although the limp usually disappears over time, leg injuries, even to fast-growing pups, can be devastating. One four-month-old female in the Mochaba pack in 1993 that sustained a broken back leg disappeared within just a few days. A three-month-old male from the Mboma pack's 1991 litter is another example: shortly before the pack moved with the pups, abandoning the den for the year, Tilt, as we later dubbed him, appeared near the den holding his neck stiffly, as if it were sore. He held

Above. *Play fighting starts at a young age, and is one of the most popular forms of play for pups. Play fighting has most of the behavioural components of real fighting, except for aggressive biting which could inflict wounds.*

Below. *A piece of impala skin keeps a pup occupied. Adult wild dogs often return to the den with a small piece of skin, which then may be used by pups to engage for hours in social play.*

his head cocked about thirty degrees to the right, a posture that seemed to force him to favour right turns. Although it became less noticeable over the following months, the tilt of his head persisted into adulthood; and although we did not observe how it happened, we have always assumed it was the result of a neck injury that occurred while he was playing.

10h50. Report from Selo at Santawane Camp: 16 lions he was following this morning ambushed a pack of dogs, probably the Santawane pack, at about 08h30 in the trees just north of White Pan, and stole its kill. Selo could not see for the dust and the action whether any dogs were killed.

I arrived at 11h20 to find vultures picking at the carcass of a female pup. Lions were lying in shade about 250 m to the south. Only one pup was found and I could not locate the rest of the pack to determine how many were missing.

Journal notes, JWM, 8 October 1994.

Some scientists have argued that the energy expended while animals are playing may be inconsequential. However, play may increase the risk of predation by lions on wild dog pups. Either because their attention is focused elsewhere or because their increased activity attracts the attention of potential predators, play can have fatal consequences. Lion predation of pups accounts

Opposite. *An alert pup chews on a grass stalk while keeping an eye on any other activities that might be more interesting. Familiarity with their environment comes from pups' recognising and distinguishing edible from inedible.*

for most of the high rate (64 per cent) of pup mortality during the first year of life. Although many fatal events may be unrelated to play, for example, when a pack is ambushed while eating at a kill, it is likely, given the amount of time pups spend playing, that some mortality occurs as a direct consequence of play. It seems a reasonable assumption that play bears some constant risks and therefore has costs, irrespective of the magnitude of its energetic output.

So what is play for? For wild dogs there is a definite developmental process in which the character and duration of play changes as dogs grow older and more powerful. This process can roughly be characterised by a progression through three stages. The first stage involves play with objects and appears to be a medium for learning about the physical world through solitary exploration and discovery. This soon evolves a social aspect in which the interest in objects derives not so much from their novelty but from their potential to stimulate social interactions. While wild dogs are very young, then, social play in its various forms becomes the most prevalent category of play and, for very young pups, play fighting the most common form of social play. In the last stage, as dogs grow larger and more powerful, play fighting declines in frequency and forms of play shift to actions that are closely related to the dogs' ecological role as efficient predators.

Object Play

Individual characters are expressed in behavioural interactions early in life for young, developing pups; character traits or dispositions such as aggressiveness or inquisitiveness are discernible among individuals from the time that they first venture from the safety of the den, at the age of five to six weeks. Some individuals seem to be more aggressive than others by nature, and direct most of their attention to interacting aggressively with litter mates, while others are more content to explore their novel physical surroundings. Developmental and genetic differences may account for some early individual differences, but environmental conditions and experiences such as those derived from play undoubtedly distil these differences into individuals with their own consistent characters.

To watch young pups investigating the limited natural world around their den, with all the novel objects that seem so significant when they are first discovered, is to witness an image of

Top. *A leopard tortoise is simply not fast enough to be of much interest for pups.*
Above left. *Olfactory overload: information from investigating a large heap of elephant dung occasionally stimulates young pups enough to taste it – but chewing faeces seems to detract from its value as a discovery fairly quickly.*
Above right. *Hooded vultures are among the first animate objects – other than other wild dogs – that pups discover in their confined world.*

Top. *Wrestling and other forms of social play are not restricted to young pups, and occasionally even adults are drawn into a short romp.*
Above. *Coyly biting at a lily, this male watches the rest of the pack playing while waiting for the right opportunity to rejoin the chase.*

Above right. *Having already eaten from the fresh kill, two adults 'box' while another watches from behind. They 'attack' each other with their mouths held loosely open, a consistent component of play fighting that changes dramatically on the rare occasions that fighting becomes real.*

innocent curiosity and genuine discovery. Later, when they leave the den and their world grows larger every day, and with accelerating speed, the wonder and investigation persist. The dogs then are using the same limited set of tools for exploration but also have a rapidly filling bank of experiences that provide some context and a few categories – such as 'dangerous' or 'not dangerous', 'edible' or 'inedible' – for an increasing familiarity with and understanding of their environment.

Much of young pups' investigations of ordinary, inanimate objects, such as old bones, sticks

and even mountains of elephant dung, around their den are experienced through the mouth, not unlike a stage in the development of children. Object play usually begins as a quiet, solo investigation of the immediate surroundings with what is presumed to be consequent instant feedback about the environment. Solo object investigation, even for particularly inquisitive young pups, seems to have limited appeal, though, compared with socially facilitated enthusiasm for the same objects. Therefore, objects such as a bone or an old, dry piece of impala skin, once prodded and

analysed, are collected and paraded proudly among the litter mates. If the treasure fails to elicit a response in the form of collective avarice from the litter mates, the apparent value of these objects declines and interest wanes rapidly.

Litter mates do, however, usually take great interest in the fact that something, novel or not, has been collected and their response is often suddenly to want the object for themselves. This initiates a common form of play among pups, which usually consists of a tug-of-war over the object. This behaviour is similar to that displayed

by adult dogs during the cooperative rending of a carcass into edible pieces, accomplished by several wild dogs pulling from the carcass in opposing directions. Even pups of four weeks old, just learning to eat meat, will aggressively tug at large scraps regurgitated for them. The play version of this feeding behaviour emphasises the strength developed by the young dogs' collectively pulling at an object, and is potentially important for developing both an awareness of cooperative feeding and the skills that will be needed to feed from a carcass beginning at an early age.

Above. *Wild dog puppies are bundles of fur, seemingly insatiable appetites on four legs. Food provides them with the energy they need.* **Right.** *Silhouetted in clouds of dust, a thirsty herd of zebra heads for a waterhole.*

Opposite, below. *The relationship between wild dogs and hyenas is complex. The consequences of interactions between them can be serious, with the hyenas often making off with a bloody back end from the dogs' sharp teeth.*

Social Play

L ife for a young wild dog pup is fairly simple. Its basic needs of food, shelter and protection are provided for by a full entourage of enthusiastic relatives in nearly constant attendance. Provided these basic requirements are met, there is little else to occupy a pup's time, so while it rapidly grows and develops, there is plenty of time for play.

Not surprisingly, play constitutes a significant portion of a wild dog pup's activities, which compels us to wonder whether it serves any useful purpose towards the development of social skills and physical coordination. Although we cannot show conclusively that meaningful social relationships are predicated on playful interactions, there is little doubt that social interactions of all kinds – and these include playful interactions – contribute to relationships with individuals that persist through time.

When pups first begin to explore the world around the mouth of the den they are particularly uncoordinated. A pup appears to be all stomach, a small, round package with four short, little legs just long enough to lift the full belly off the ground – very young wild dog pups appear to be little more than small support systems for their stomachs: it seems they need the head only for the mouth, to get food to the stomach, and the legs only to get to the food. Much of young pups' locomotion is punctuated by the predictable effects of gravity on a round object, and the pups spend much time rolling down any small incline such as a pile of sand or backwards into the mouth of the den. As they grow, their locomotor coordination develops, and they very soon begin engaging in short bouts of physically demanding social play.

There are numerous forms of social play which partially mimic adult social interactions with important life-history consequences.

Perhaps the most common of these is play fighting. Play fighting with litter mates includes biting, tackling, wrestling, and aggressive vocalisations such as growls and yips. Not only are social reactions and interactions in play fighting potentially important for learning about and establishing relationships with litter mates, but we assume that the skills and motor coordination needed for these same playful interactions are being developed at the same time.

Most components of 'real' fighting are present in play fighting, except those that typically lead to the infliction of injury on an opponent. In African wild dogs, and other canids such as wolves, coyotes and domestic dogs, most play fighting is characterised by the mouths of the players being held wide open, so that aggres-

sive attack behaviours such as biting and tearing are noticeably absent.

The reversal of the role of winner and loser in play fights is also common at young ages, but as the pups grow older and develop greater strength and coordination this bilateral component may change and become unilateral, with only one individual of any given pair consistently playing the winner. Differences in the amount and form of play fighting between the genders have been recorded for several species of mammals but studies of coyotes and wolves found no such differences, and we have found no consistent differences between male and female wild dogs. Males seem to play fight just as frequently as females, and choice of play partners appears to be independent of gender.

Right. *Sibling relationships might last, depending on dispersal, throughout a dog's life. These are reinforced by constant, close social contact.*
Far right. *By the age of five months, pups have developed considerable strength and coordination which can be seen in the increased speed and agility of their energetic play.*

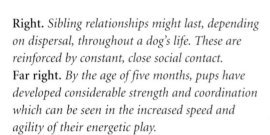

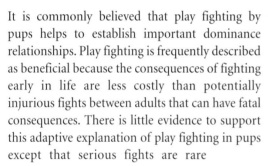

It is commonly believed that play fighting by pups helps to establish important dominance relationships. Play fighting is frequently described as beneficial because the consequences of fighting early in life are less costly than potentially injurious fights between adults that can have fatal consequences. There is little evidence to support this adaptive explanation of play fighting in pups except that serious fights are rare

events between adult siblings that are potential contestants for dominance and access to mates. However, serious fights do occur (albeit rarely) between adults, and occasionally between adult litter mates that have grown up and played together their entire lives (see Chapter One). This indicates that dominance relationships are not necessarily fully resolved when the dogs are pups, and also that they are able to resolve them as adults, by fighting.

Furthermore, unequivocal dominance relationships between non-litter mate siblings are very common between males in emigrating groups, and although non-litter mates sometimes play together, they rarely engage in play fighting. Therefore, it is worth noting that a history of play fighting as pups is neither necessary nor sufficient for wild dogs to settle the question of dominance in lifelong relationships.

Chase Play

Play is predominantly a recreation for the young at heart – for wild dogs less than two years old. The disposition, type and duration of play all change as the dogs grow older. In general, as dogs age they play less frequently and for shorter periods and, although they occasionally live to

be more than ten years old, they seldom play after the age of three.

Occasionally, however, older wild dogs do get an itch to be included in a game; when they do, it is almost exclusively a form of social play called chase play, a game of 'tag' that involves simply chasing others, typically through shallow rainwater pans. In fact, it appears to be the opportunity to run splashing through water without concern for crocodiles that most often motivates chase play. This is yet another form of social play which involves the individual's speed and coordination, and almost certainly facilitates developing skills. It provides a context for experience, to practise chasing, and, perhaps most importantly, an opportunity to learn the effects of chasing something as a collective group. This form of play has distinct similarities to the hunting and capturing behaviour of wild dogs when they hunt prey.

Even old wild dogs occasionally are swept up in the spirit of chase play and participate briefly with the younger ones that initiate it, as if momentarily forgetting their age and their

aches and pains. For the young dogs the game will continue sometimes for several minutes, until they tire and lie down.

07h20. When I arrived, the Mababe pack was just finishing this morning's kill, an adult male impala, about 150 m up Khwai River from the cut-line crossing. Snooker, beginning to look pregnant, left the kill along with Poker and the rest, except for the three older females, Bridge, Gin and Croquet, who stayed back for a couple of minutes picking at what was left of the carcass.

They trotted off through the scrub to the southeast and within about 500 m ran into a group of 12 wildebeest, including two juveniles. All seven yearlings started for them immediately, almost encircling them from about 30-40 m away. The others lay down and watched as the wildebeest spun and chased the yearlings, all of which were full from having eaten just half an hour earlier.

Journal notes, JWM, 17 April 1991.

Fully grown zebra and wildebeest are frequently listed as prey items for the wild dogs that historically inhabited the Serengeti Plains of East Africa. In Botswana adults of these and other large ungulate species are rarely, if ever, considered potential

prey by experienced wild dogs. However, it is common for a pack of dogs suddenly to stop what it is doing and engage a small group of ten to twenty wildebeest, zebra or buffalo in what appears to be a probing precursor to a hunt. Curiously, only some of the wild dogs approach the herd, while others simply lie down and watch.

The 'prey' typically stand facing the approaching dogs, snorting and stomping, in a tight mob, until one charges the dogs and chases them off. This is repeated as the dogs run just far away enough for the chase to stop, and then return to be chased again. This appears to be related to a hunting attempt but seldom amounts to more than a high-risk game of 'dare'.

Virtually all the dogs that indulge in this game are yearlings or younger, while the older dogs are the ones that lie in the distance, as if being entertained by the action. Some dogs seem to underestimate the speed and turning ability

Opposite. *Two pups tussle over a piece of grass.*
Above. *During the few months of the rainy season, the rich browns of a wild dog's otherwise cryptic patterns and colours are sharply contrasted against the deep green grass.*

Above. *Three litter mates find a terrapin a curiosity worthy of cautious inspection. When flood plains dry out, terrapins are sometimes abandoned in dried-up pools and must make their way overland to find a new home.*
Left. *There is no love lost on wild dogs by elephants. Juveniles sometimes take advantage of the elephants' reactions by playfully harassing them, usually eliciting a charge and an angry trumpet that sends the dogs running.*
Opposite. *An old flattened termite mound provides yet another opportunity for social play, this one involving an elevated vantage point in an otherwise entirely flat landscape.*

of a charging bull and we have seen some bold yearlings come extremely close to being injured by the horns of an aggressive wildebeest or buffalo or kicked by the powerful hooves of a zebra stallion.

While this form of behaviour involves considerable risk to the dogs indulging in it, and has the components of a serious hunting attempt, we regard it as a developed form of chase play in which only older juveniles engage.

We have seen the same wild dog behaviour directed at small groups of giraffe and elephant, suggesting strongly that young dogs (those less than two years old) are inclined simply to chasing everything and anything that looks like it might run from them.

Healthy Dogs Play

Play at any level of intensity suggests that the players' perception of their world is not immutably serious, significant or life threatening, that there is energy to spend having fun and opportunity for the extravagance. Observing wild dogs at play is undeniably a pleasant, 'feel-good' wildlife experience for anybody with the good fortune to be able to watch. Their naturally relaxed enthusiasm is contagious and communicates something directly to us about the state of their world – play behaviour is an important indicator of the animals' general health.

The nutritional status of wild dog pups early in their lives can be related only to the amount and quality of milk they are able to glean from their mother. Later, as they are weaned, their growth and general health will depend largely upon the ability of the rest of the pack to provision them with regurgitated meat. During both of these periods of early development the resources available to each pup are also dependent on the number of pups in the litter. Litter sizes of wild dogs are extremely large compared with other large canid species like wolves and coyotes. In Botswana the average annual litter size is ten pups, and we have seen as many as 16 pups in a litter successfully raised by a pack. (Even larger litters have been reported; one female in the Kruger National Park, South Africa was reported to have 19 pups in a single litter.)

Above left. *Chasing vultures always elicits a response and, although adults appear to try, they seldom catch one. Vultures are common uninvited guests at wild dog kills but seem to pose no threat.*
Left. *An adult wild dog leaps energetically through the water. When animals are in poor condition or poor health, play behaviour is the first to be eliminated.*
Above right. *Yearlings seem to enjoy the sport of harassing wildebeest.*

The ability to adequately provision that many pups indicates that the habitat supports suitable prey densities for the dogs to regularly and reliably return to the den with food. If the habitat is less than optimal, and the availability of suitable prey is inadequate for the pack, the den and the pups might be abandoned. We have never observed such food stress in northern Botswana, but it has been reported in the Serengeti where wild dogs were relying heavily on a migratory population of wildebeest for prey.

All animals can be said to be on an energy budget, and in animal behaviour scientists have always assumed that animals prioritise their behaviour based on the behaviour's probable benefits and costs. Play, which according to our definition has no immediate function but carries at least some specific energetic cost, would have to be considered a low budget priority.

Consistent with this assumption is the fact that play behaviour is commonly related to the health and the nutritional status of domestic animals. Indeed, in veterinary medicine a frequent query into the health of a domestic animal is whether there has been a change in the patient's willingness to engage in play. When animals are in poor condition or poor health, and are generally not feeling well, play behaviour is the first to be eliminated. Therefore, animals whose health is compromised or whose energy levels are low are not expected to play. On the other hand, individuals that play exhaustively can be assumed to be in relatively good health and nutritionally fit.

Energetic play is a positive indicator not only of general nutritional fitness, it also gives reasonable assurance that the animals are not

Left. *To taste is to explore, and even chewing a twig can be an outlet to ward off the dulling effects of an uneventful afternoon while waiting until the rest of the pack gets up to go hunting again.*
Below. *A trio of pups, at younger than three months old, finds almost everything to be a novelty and meritorious of some collective investigation.*
Right. *In the middle of a deep-water crossing, the dogs are just able to reach the bottom to push through without swimming. Regular crossings of the clear waters of the Okavango Delta may be risky for the dogs, but it probably helps to keep them clean and free of some parasites.*

experiencing any ill effects from disease. Disease in wild dogs is an important conservation consideration, because wild dogs are susceptible to numerous lethal diseases common to domestic dogs. Furthermore, the constant social contact between all wild dogs in a pack means that any virus, once started in a pack, will quickly and effectively spread to all the dogs in the pack.

Wild dog populations in Tanzania and Kenya were decimated by diseases during the recent past. In 1990 a rabies virus infected the wild dogs of the Serengeti and Masai Mara, and nearly half of the packs known in those areas died out in a few weeks. The following year the rest of the known populations in those areas disappeared entirely, and evidence indicates that a canine distemper virus, originating from the domestic dog population in the area, was responsible for the second and final epidemic. We have recorded only infrequent contact with these diseases in our study of the wild dogs of northern Botswana to date, but in 1994 at least one pack died of distemper, in the Chobe district, and the threat of disease is increasing throughout the region.

Of all the active social interactions in Botswana's population of African wild dogs, the social behaviour of play has the most significance in terms of the general long-term health and viability of the region's wild dog population. We can be reassured of the dogs' continuing health if we continue regularly to observe wildly energetic play.

Predator

What if wild dogs ate only grass?

We were once told by a local entrepreneur high in the Karakoram Mountains of northern Pakistan that snow leopards (*Panthera uncia*) were wrongly persecuted by people as predators of goats and sheep. This experienced old resident explained in all seriousness, and in a conspiratorial whisper that clearly marked him among the knowledgeable few, that 'snow leopards eat only grass'.

How he came by this interesting piece of information is a mystery, but a similar perception of wild dogs in Africa could have interesting consequences. We have often wondered whether the negative images that have accompanied African wild dogs throughout their history in association with humans can be attributed solely to the fact that they are carnivorous. Do they suffer persecution at the hand of modern man, irrespective of their diet, simply because they are dogs?

Although this is (at least for some) an interesting philosophical question which needles at our deepest, probably unconscious perceptions of wild canids in general, it is somewhat moot because wild dogs do not, of course, eat grass. *Lycaon pictus* is a member of the taxonomic Order Carnivora, together with lions, leopards, cheetahs, jackals, foxes, hyenas, honey badgers, mongooses, and many others. Of these carnivores, some are opportunists and generalists that will eat anything from termites and beetles to whatever they can pull from an old elephant carcass. Wild dogs, however, eat fresh meat and virtually nothing else.

The fact that wild dogs hunt effectively and efficiently as a group has doubtless contributed to the persistent perceptions of them as malevolent killers. A pack of wild dogs stalking silently across a flood plain in the golden light of an African evening might unfortunately be likened to a gang of errant youths, hoodlums whose toughness derives from the fact that they are in a group, a social collection of 'bad attitudes'. The image evokes the conclusion that in a properly ordered world these gangs would not exist. The group hunting behaviour of wild dogs is neither errant nor 'good' or 'bad', however. African wild dogs are not feral dogs, or 'good' dogs gone 'bad', but merely the results of a fairly

Previous page, left. *A couple of dogs attempt to tear open the hide of a young buffalo calf they have killed at night. Wild dogs shift their schedule for a short period every month, to hunt during nights when the moon is bright.*
Previous page, right. *Although dogs rely on vision for their hunting and travelling, it is not uncommon to find them moving in what appears to be complete darkness.*

This page. *Caught at the edge of a flood plain in shallow water, a lechwe falls prey to a skilful hunting pack. Adult male lechwe are larger-than-average prey for wild dogs, but dogs can become quite skilled at capturing them, even in shallow water, where they usually escape from other predators. Once the wild dogs have pulled down the lechwe, they dispatch it quickly, and collectively drag the carcass to dry ground.*

successful response in an evolutionary sense to the challenges of making a living in an unforgiving African landscape.

The fact that wild dogs are predators is probably the best known bit of general knowledge about their natural behaviour. Until recently, however, wild dog predatory behaviour had not been critically researched from the point of view of evolutionary adaptation or their unique role in the environment.

Wild dogs are specialist predators that hunt medium-sized ruminants. In northern Botswana

the most common medium-sized ruminant, impala, constitutes approximately 80 to 85 per cent of the diet of most wild dog packs.

African wild dogs also occasionally and opportunistically hunt several other species of antelope, including red lechwe, reedbuck and steenbok, and the calves or juveniles of some of the larger species, including kudu, tsessebe, wildebeest, zebra and buffalo. How they accomplish this capture of an animal usually several times their size is a remarkable example of swift efficiency and teamwork.

The pack is essential to the wild dog's hunting success, since a single dog cannot bring down large prey.

JW Sheldon. Wild Dogs: The Natural History of the Nondomestic Canidae, *Academic Press, San Diego, 1992.*

Many have explained pack social organisation in terms of an assumed need for several dogs to kill their relatively large prey. We have observed numerous kills by single individuals, however, and know further of one adult female that lived

alone for more than eight months, regularly preying on impala to feed herself, just as she would have done had she been living in a pack. Although it could be said that a large group size enables wild dogs to prey on some larger species, such as zebra and wildebeest, we find no evidence to support the assertion that dogs must live in packs to successfully capture prey or that the primary function of pack living is to capture large prey. A typical prey capture in Botswana might involve anything from one to several wild dogs, but the vast majority of their prey – impala

Opposite. *A sub-adult male lion proudly displays its healthy canines in a gaping yawn. Lions are responsible for the vast majority of natural wild dog mortality in northern Botswana, and figure significantly in the dogs' natural history.*
Above. *Evening shade settles on a small herd of Burchell's zebra. A species of open grasslands, zebra group together in small family herds.*

and other small to medium-sized antelope – is not so large that more than one dog is required to capture it.

A complete understanding of African wild dog hunting behaviour requires an appreciation of the high risk of potentially fatal injury associated with hunting and an explanation of the underlying social structure that dictates which individual wild dogs are likely to be the hungriest. The latter determines how and why some individuals are relatively more motivated than others to take those risks.

A full description of their hunting behaviour on a typical day in the life of an African wild dog pack should help dispel some common misconceptions of wild dogs as ravenous and ruthless predators. Wild dogs' active periods are during the crepuscular hours of the day – early morning and late evening. No two days are exactly the same for a pack of wild dogs but very important rituals and routines are consistently observed by all healthy packs, that define and organise each day's activities; and these activities are all fundamentally related to the need to regularly acquire enough to eat.

Ritual

At the first signs of dawn's light the day begins for wild dogs. Varying only somewhat with the weather and their level of hunger, a ritualised social frenzy in preparation for the hunt gets the wild dog day off to a jump start. 'Wake-up' is usually initiated by the individual that ate the least from the last kill and, depending on the motivation of the others, getting the rest of the pack started might require patience by the hungriest ones. Typically, one will initiate the

pre-hunting greeting ritual by standing, stretching and casting a look about to see where the rest of the pack is lying. The others may lift their heads, watch and roll over or they may jump up and help get the production started.

Occasionally, the dominant female will initiate the greeting ceremony, particularly if the pack has been at the den for several weeks and the pups are getting older. She may well be weary of the same scenery, of begging for regurgitated food from other adults; she may be eager to stretch her legs or be anxious to have a chance to eat her own meal without having to wait for another dog to regurgitate it for her. Sometimes one of the younger dogs in the pack will simply become anxious or bored with resting and lying about. However, it is usually a subordinate adult that initiates the wake-up ritual. This is because the subordinate adults and older (two- and three-year-old) offspring from the pack are usually the hungriest, and therefore the most motivated to hunt. Why some are more motivated than others is related to the coordinated and strictly organised hierarchical system of feeding priority observed by all the pack members at a kill.

As the entire pack wakes and rallies, the activity level increases. What appears be a canid pep rally, with considerable whining and twittering,

physical contact, playing and general excitement, may have several important functions, including cementing social bonds between pack members, reinforcing dominant and subordinate social relationships and ensuring the presence of all pack members who might be lying somewhere in the near distance. For the youngest set, it seems the event is like a party: they bustle around chasing each other and the adults, and sometimes they even get their older siblings to play with them. For all of the dogs the ritual seems to awaken and alert all to a change in pack activity.

Following the greeting, the pack heads out in what appears to be a random direction, and the morning hunt sequence is under way, occurring as it has been since long before the presence of man in the African environment.

The Hunt

The pack sets out after the greeting ceremony at a walking pace, like starting in first gear to get some momentum. The dogs ramble through the bush for the first few minutes, usually in a dispersed file, following a lead dog, typically an experienced, older adult. If they see any prey at this early stage, they will often merely watch it until it runs off, as if they know they cannot shift

from first into fourth gear without some warm-up.

As the hunt progresses, the dogs shift into second gear, a steady trot which is an easy, relaxed gait that gives the impression they could travel forever without tiring. They seem to be loosening up in this trot and, moving at approximately four to six kilometres per hour, they begin to cover some distance. After a few minutes at this pace comes another shift of gait, a slow, easy, loping run which indicates their readiness to seriously pursue any potential prey they might encounter.

If at any time up to this stage the wild dogs encounter any game animals, including some of the larger species of prey such as wildebeest,

Opposite. *The dying light and dust-filled air obscure the to-and-fro drama between a herd of buffalo and a pack of wild dogs. A single bull stands ready to run the dogs off.*

Above. *In striking contrast to the backlit sky, oxpeckers take to the air above a jostling herd of buffalo focused on grazing in the thick grasses of the Okavango's seasonal flood plains.*

Right. *A total of 24 adult dogs ate from this buffalo carcass. It is unlikely that the dogs killed it; because of their number, they could have pirated it from a small group of lions or hyenas.*

zebra or waterbuck, a group of dogs might split from the lead dogs and try to give chase. This will invariably be a group of young, inexperienced yearlings which will chase almost anything that will react to them, including giraffe and elephant. However, these species are typically unimpressed by wild dogs harassing them, and simply form a tight mob and hold their ground. A stallion or bull from a threatened group may chase the young dogs with repeated aggressive charges that would severely injure them if they were too slow to run away. The older, more experienced adults will wait for a while and watch before pressing on to find more suitable prey.

Wild dogs have a formation that they follow when hunting. It's always the furry ones that lead, and they stay in a line. When the front one gets tired the next one takes over and the front one drops to the back of the line. That way they are always strong.
Interview, LPB, 30 July 1995.

Descriptions of wild dog hunting behaviour have commonly included some impression that hunting groups of dogs cooperate, on the basis of some collective strategy, to capture their prey.

The question of whether wild dogs hunt cooperatively is far from resolved, however. Most accounts of wild dogs capturing prey describe how a group systematically rotates the leader in the chase, keeping a fresh runner near the front to relieve the leader as it tires. However, this description lacks empirical credibility because it is not obvious why a leading wild dog would be more tired than the dog that would need to be right behind it to take over the chase.

What does occur, and what has undoubtedly led to this interpretation of their hunting behaviour, is that pursued antelope often turn abruptly to change direction, either simply to attempt to escape or to avoid running into a completely unfamiliar area. Whatever the reason, when an animal changes direction while being chased by several predators strung out in pursuit, simple geometry can result in dogs that were behind the leader suddenly finding themselves closer to the intended prey and therefore in the lead. This could happen several times in chases involving several dogs and in relatively open habitat. In this sense, pack mates often share in the capture of a single prey, but they do not cooperate or create strategies for hunting. Their hunting technique may more accurately be

described as opportunistic, in the sense that they hunt as individuals with a common objective and respond opportunistically to changing conditions in the most effective way possible.

Once a group of impala has been spotted by the lead dogs they stop and watch them as the rest of the pack assembles around them. The dogs then silently spread out, focusing intently on the impala ahead. In a wide front they begin stalking, each with the head held low, keeping an eye out for what the others are doing and at the same time trying to avoid missing any moves by the group of impala. The chase begins only when the impala, upon seeing the dogs, take fright, snort and eventually break into a run. At this point everything shifts into high gear, and the chase becomes very fast and difficult to follow.

Wild dogs are said to have been recorded moving at speeds in excess of 60 kilometres per hour while chasing prey and we have no evidence to suggest this statistic is not accurate. Several dogs might chase a single impala or, more commonly, several impala are chased individually by some of the lead dogs. Within only a few seconds an experienced dog will stop a chase if it sees there is little chance of catching the prey. If, however, a chase continues through broken woodlands, bush and open areas it could continue for several hundred metres; in open habitats like the short-grass plains of parts of East Africa, chases have been recorded that continued for several kilometres. In the Okavango Delta, where the habitat is characterised by broken woodland patches interspersed with small, grassy

and seasonally inundated flood plains, wild dogs rarely chase prey for more than a kilometre, and most kills are made within 600 to 800 metres of where the chase began.

If any single aspect of wild dog hunting behaviour has generated a gross distortion of their image as predators in the ecosystem, it is the method by which wild dogs dispatch their prey. They have been described as eating their prey while it is still alive (see Prologue), running beside prey while tearing chunks from it until it falls, and so forth. It is clearly in the best interests of the wild dogs to kill their prey quickly, because wild dogs are small relative to most of their prey, and they risk serious injury from the dangerous hooves and horns of the struggling animal. This is especially true in southern Africa since it is

Above. *The pack heads off on the afternoon hunt at a relaxed, steady trot, raising only a whisper of dust as it moves. The dogs average more than ten kilometres in a day.*
Opposite. *With piercing, amber eyes and an aloof stare, a leopard casually drinks from a drying pool.*

not uncommon for wild dogs in the subregion to capture prey alone, single handed.

The killing by wild dogs of an average-sized antelope is consistently and swiftly accomplished by disembowelment. Larger prey might require more time to wrestle down and tear into, but the method of disembowelling is the same: the dogs tear with their knife-like teeth into the soft part of the belly of their prey and extract the vital organs – liver, heart and lungs – with almost surgical precision and lightning speed, thereby killing the prey in a matter of seconds. Once the rest of the pack arrives the carcass is often dismembered in seconds, the dogs working with team-like coordination.

With so many individuals splitting from the pack during a hunt and heading in separate directions at full speed, it is not unusual for a hunter occasionally to be separated from the group and lose contact with the pack. After trying unsuccessfully for several minutes to locate its pack, a separated dog will begin calling for its mates. The call is variously described as a 'hoo' call, or functionally as a location or contact call. It sounds

more like an owl or a loud dove call than a sound one would expect from a large carnivore. It carries in normal habitat and conditions for at least two kilometres and gives precise information about the caller's location and, probably, individual identity as well. When the pack hears the calls of a separated pack member, it either responds with 'hoo' calls to announce its location, or it runs in the direction of the caller until they reunite.

If a hunter is unsuccessful, it returns to where the hunt began. There the rest of the pack is usually anxiously awaiting its arrival, eager to learn the outcome of the hunt. An unsuccessful hunter is greeted only briefly and allowed to lie down with the others.

Upon the return of a successful hunter, however, the pack winds up with great enthusiasm and excitement, especially the youngest dogs, which beg relentlessly for the hunter to regurgitate some meat to them. Often the only recourse available to the returning hunter to stop the harassment is to regurgitate some meat and move away quickly while the group of juveniles tussles over the food. After a short rest, possibly to

wait for any other missing hunters, the hunter then quietly leads the others directly back to the site of the kill.

Cooperation

Once back at the kill, a surprising lack of noise prevails. While the adults spread out in a fan from the carcass several metres away, facing outwards to watch out for pirating hyenas or ambushing lions, only the young pups of the year feed from the kill – wild dogs consistently favour their youngest members by yielding to them priority access to food. This priority of access to

the kill given to the youngest in the group is unlike social behaviour practised by most other large carnivores but wild dog pups have no trouble dictating their authority over their older relatives because they are supported by the dominant pair. The pups use their sharp teeth on the muzzles of their elders if they have not yet satisfied their prodigious appetites.

It is remarkable to watch four- or five-month-old wild dog pups aggressively seeing off older, and sometimes fully adult, siblings which, if they resist, are reprimanded severely by the dominant pair. The pups are always the first to be given access to a kill. Yearlings have the 'second

sitting', then two-year-olds, before the oldest subordinate adults finally have their turn at whatever remains.

The dominant pair in a pack seems to be able to eat more or less at will, usually stepping in after the pups have finished. They also actively enforce the priority-of-access rules, making sure elders wait their turn if necessary. What this means is that the oldest offspring from the pack and the subordinate adults are always last to gain access to a carcass. If the pack is large, and particularly if there are many pups to feed, the older wild dogs may sometimes end up with nothing more than a bone on which to chew.

Left. *With only the white tip of its tail giving it away, an immaculately camouflaged young male leopard walks through a wooded island.*
Above. *It is not uncommon for a group of young dogs from a pack to engage a small herd of zebra in a form of chase play that appears related to a hunting attempt. In Botswana, zebra are rarely eaten by wild dogs and usually merely chase the dogs away.*
Below. *Indulging its natural curiosity, this wild dog stopped by camp one evening to check in and see what was cooking. Caught in the flash, it momentarily looked a little uncertain about the noise from the camera.*

This differential access to a kill results in differing levels of motivation among the older adults of the pack for the following hunting period. Only if these older adults actually make a kill single-handed can they eat what they want, uncontested, because there are few or no other dogs present. This would account for why successful hunters sometimes delay for several minutes before returning to collect the rest of the pack and leading them to their kill. Subordinate adults are therefore motivated by hunger, as a result of a social system that cedes priority access to food to the youngest pack members first, often resulting in the oldest getting very little.

Risk and Motivation

In their natal pack, young dogs gain experience and learn the essentials for independent survival with a buffer against the effects of failures and mistakes provided by the experience of their older pack mates. Young dogs do not begin hunting with any degree of success until they are almost a year old; most individuals that survive to two years can be considered accomplished hunters. The training period also includes important experience in how to avoid ambush by lions. This experience is just as important as hunting skills for a wild dog's future success in a new pack.

The role of the subordinate adults, usually the founding pack members and siblings to the dominant pair, in this regard is integral to the success of the pack's offspring. It is these dogs that represent the cornerstone of the pack, filling the roles of both teacher and provider. These individuals seldom emigrate, remaining as non-breeding adults with their dominant siblings.

Left, top to bottom. *With their quickness and agility, wild dogs typically dance around a hyena, inflicting stinging bites to its backside. Dogs are usually able to guard their kill from hyenas, depending on how many hyenas there are; if a clan starts to arrive in numbers, however, the dogs begrudgingly concede their kill to the pirates.* **Right.** *The soft, dog-like features of this spotted hyena belie its extremely powerful jaws, adapted for crushing bones. Although sometimes mistaken for dogs, spotted hyenas are more closely related to the cats than to the dog family.*

A pack can be severely compromised if an older subordinate adult and key hunter for the pack is killed because these individuals take a disproportionate share of the life-threatening risks associated with hunting for the rest of the pack.

17h35. The Santawane pack, all eight pups present, under an acacia at the edge of Lechwe Plain. Greeting, at 17h25, was initiated by Singha, but then they all lay down again.

17h47. Tetly and Singha started to walk away, on hunt, to the west across the flood plain. The others followed, but the pups were strung out at least 100 m behind the leaders. Tetly initiated a chase on a group of impala from about 180 m away, mid flood plain. Several were chased across the track in front of me but a large cloud of dust rose back near where the hunt had started as if something had been caught there.

I arrived and found Fetch hobbling, with a bleeding compound fracture of the left femur. What happened? There are spring-hare holes everywhere, but I find it difficult to believe, after all these years . . .
Journal entry, JWM, 16 October 1995.

Hunting – chasing prey at high speeds through bush and tall grass – is an extremely high-risk enterprise for wild dogs. The countless number of leg injuries that can directly be attributed to hunting accidents has impressed upon us the significance of the priority-of-access system for subordinate wild dogs compared to dominants.

Leg injury is the second highest source of natural mortality for wild dogs, second only to lion-caused mortality, the risk of which is also increased during hunting.

Therefore, the social practice which provides priority access to kills for the pack's youngest members is a cost in terms of the increasing risks for those older and lower-priority individuals

which, in order to eat, may be forced to go out and catch something for themselves.

Hunting Success

The rate of successful hunts by wild dogs is a measure of interest to nearly anybody who has observed them, from animal researchers and wildlife managers to general wildlife enthusiasts. Hunting success is a statistic which, if it could be measured accurately, would facilitate a comparison of different packs of wild dogs or different species of predators and could be of fundamental importance in scientifically analysing the evolution of their social behaviour. Measuring hunting success is more difficult than it sounds, however.

In fact, from the point of view of field research it can be a veritable nightmare because it is not obvious how it should be measured. For example, are wild dogs that kill a lechwe more successful than those that kill a steenbok? The answer could depend on the number of dogs hunting, the number of dogs eating, the frequency of previous and future kills, and the size, age, condition and density

of potential prey. It could also depend on the distance travelled, the number of animals chased, the duration of the hunt and the habitat type.

Wild dogs are known to be efficient predators, but with all the variables involved, how efficient is not an easily quantifiable concept. Reports have estimated the hunting success rate for an average group of wild dogs variously from 33 to 85 per cent. We have found that an average pack successfully kills a full-sized antelope about once in every three times that it gets up from resting to travel, which is the only time it is inclined to hunt. In other words, wild dogs kill an average of two impala every three days (since they move twice nearly every day), which gives a hunting success of 33 per cent for an average pack.

Obviously, larger packs of wild dogs must acquire more food than smaller packs to provide enough for all the pack members to eat. From the point of view of provisioning a group from a single carcass, there appears to be a threshold

Opposite. *The smallest of the large African cats, cheetahs are the only other diurnal large carnivore and, because they also prey on small and medium-sized antelopes, they compete directly with wild dogs.*
Above. *A small herd of lechwe finds refuge in the watery expanse of an Okavango flood plain. Their solidly built hindquarters enable lechwe to*

bound through water and marshy terrain with relative ease, usually leaving their comparatively cumbersome predators behind.
Right. *The scene at a wild dog kill is quiet and surprisingly orderly. There is a strict order of access to the kill based on age, with the youngest dogs eating first, while the older, subordinate adults wait to pick at what remains.*

pack size above which diminishing meal sizes for some individuals result. This pack size seems to be about eight to ten adult dogs. In northern Botswana the most common prey for wild dogs is impala, of which an average-sized adult appears to feed eight to ten dogs. At this group size nothing is wasted, but as the pack grows larger, some dogs might occasionally go hungry.

As a pack grows significantly larger, and reaches 16 to 20 members, we expect regularly to

see double the rate of kills made to sustain the pack. This presents a constraint on the otherwise consistent social cohesion of the pack because not all pack members might eat at the same place or necessarily at the same time. In order not to completely splinter the pack into hunting groups which might lose track of each other for varying periods of time, not only does there need to be a high prey density, but dogs have to be motivated to hunt independently of their pack mates.

Left. *On the move again, a group of hunting dogs trudges through the dry bushveld. Although a typical pack of wild dogs will hunt every morning and evening, the dogs are not successful in every attempt.*
Below left. *A group of adults tugs on the ear of a young buffalo calf which was systematically weeded out from the rest of the herd.*
Opposite. *As if sculpted, the set of horns of one alert buffalo is sharply contrasted against the blood-red African sky.*

Those that end up with nothing to eat from the remains of a carcass are, predictably, older siblings and subordinate adults, and these are the dogs that commonly form smaller hunting groups.

Once wild dogs have captured and killed something to eat, they are susceptible to losing their meal to pirating lions and hyenas. Spotted hyenas will pirate kills from other animals whenever they get the chance, and wild dogs are one of their favourite targets. Wild dogs and hyenas in a stand-off over a carcass must weigh the odds and decide when to contest and when to concede. At only a third the weight of a spotted hyena, a wild dog must rely on strength in numbers. Defending a kill against hyenas seems to have predictable results based on the numbers of members in each group. The number that favours wild dogs in such contests is approximately four dogs for each hyena, up to four hyenas, above which number hyenas seem to overpower most packs of dogs.

Particularly bold hyenas on occasion do succeed in pirating a carcass but this depends on how much of the carcass remains. If the dogs have eaten most of it, they are not motivated to defend it from an insistent hyena, probably because engaging hyenas physically is not without risk of injury for wild dogs. Hyenas have been known to attack and kill adult dogs in Botswana, but lone hyenas are commonly chased, attacked and harried away by wild dogs which bite their backsides and appear to be unimpressed with the snapping, vice-like jaws of the bloodied hyena.

Defending a kill from lions is a different story. Lion ambush, which often occurs at a kill, is a significant cause of wild dog mortality, and African wild dogs seldom resist even a single lion when challenged for their kill. A lion can maim a dog fatally with a single swipe of a paw, so the risk of defending a carcass against a marauding lion is significant. Wild dogs when faced with a lion ambush have little choice but to surrender their food and retreat with an opportunity to hunt again.

During a typical day in the life of a wild dog, the middle of the day is spent resting. If it is hot they spread out to take advantage of whatever shade can be found under the various trees of the region. These are typically knobthorn, camel-thorn or mopane trees; if they are deep in the delta where the riparian edge provides water to support large, sweeping shade trees, the dogs relax under the luxurious shade of an old sycamore fig or an ebony. On a cold or rainy day they will curl up together in a heap, draping heads and paws over each other and trying to squeeze in between others to keep warm. They get up occasionally to stretch, change positions, relocate as the sun moves or ramble to a nearby pan for a drink of water. For the most part, however, they do not go anywhere or do anything of significance through the middle of the day, which is spent largely in attentive but relaxed rest until, in the lengthening evening light, one of them initiates the ritual of waking and greeting, and the hunt begins again.

Wild dogs are predators only when they are hungry and hunting, and that is only for a small portion of each day. They are highly skilled and efficient predators, but after hunting during the first and last couple of daylight hours, they are like any other drowsy dogs. For the remainder of the time, their behaviour is almost contrary to what we typically imagine when we think of predators. Wild dogs are not aggressive towards humans, as evidenced by the fact that there has never been a reliable account of wild dogs attacking or injuring a person (see Chapter Five).

Wild dogs work hard and play hard; they respect each other; they cooperate to raise young and protect themselves from predators; and they are highly effective hunters. All of these characteristics should command awe and respect by all human standards. Perhaps only a deeper look into our unconscious responses to wild canids and our long history of close association with their domestic cousins will truly reveal the causes of the persistent and inappropriate malevolence harboured for these wild predators.

Prey

In nature there are two fundamental explanations for why animals live in groups:

to improve the amount or quality of what they eat and

to decrease the probability of being eaten.

≈

In the continuum that is widely known as the food chain, to eat and avoid being eaten are fundamental organising principles of animal behaviour. This applies to wild dogs as much as it does to the prey species from which they make their living. Wild dogs are merely a link in the chain, players among the many living things that eat other living things, whether plant or animal, while simultaneously trying to avoid the same fate. As is the case with all living things, the influence of wild dogs' predation has shaped, through time and evolution, the biological and ecological character, behaviour and social organisation of the living things on which they prey.

Although wild dogs in Botswana prey primarily on impala, their historical distribution in widely varying habitats throughout sub-Saharan Africa attests to their catholic and adaptable nature. Wild dogs prefer to hunt medium-sized antelope where these are available, but they are capable of adapting to widely varying conditions of prey-species availability. They have been known to prey on scrub hares, large birds, warthogs and zebras, and most if not all species in the family Bovidae, which includes all the antelopes (and if not the adults of these species then, at least occasionally, their calves). Under conditions of extreme food stress, which occur sometimes in habitats with low prey densities, wild dogs will occasionally even eat carrion.

Presented in publications, from the earliest explorers' accounts to modern compilations of wildlife photographs, as tireless cursorial predators of speedy gazelles in open, short-grass plains, wild dogs have captured the imagination of armchair travellers around the world for more than a hundred years. They unwittingly became a symbol of what was not only wild but particularly disorderly in the untamed

Previous page, left. *An adult male lechwe is pulled down by a large pack. In the middle of the delta densities of lechwe are even higher than those of impala, and the packs of wild dogs that live in these areas become quite skilled at hunting in the shallow floodwaters.*

Previous page, right. *A single female impala, the most frequent prey species of wild dogs in Botswana, is particularly alert as it ventures out of the nearby woodland edge to graze.*

nether lands of Africa. Stories and photographs commonly depicted wild dogs as sensational cooperative predators of larger game animals such as wildebeest and zebra – creatures almost ten times their weight.

Graphic photographs of wild dogs pulling down zebra and adult wildebeest in the short-grass plains are, however, less illustrative of their typical predatory behaviour than they are of their ability to adapt to conditions of prey availability and habitats that are less than optimal.

Our collective general perception of African wild dogs as predators of the plains has evolved considerably since early accounts presented them as a pestilence in the otherwise stable balance

of nature. For example, based on where the remaining few wild dog populations persist and thrive today (in Tanzania, South Africa and across northern Botswana into southwestern Zimbabwe), and based on our more detailed understanding of their ecology as extremely adaptable carnivores, we have concluded that savannah woodland, broken woodland and scrub habitats should be considered optimal habitats for African wild dogs.

Shifting slightly our perceptions of wild dogs from open-plains predators to predators of savannah-woodland habitats changes significantly the way we think about the relationships between African wild dogs and the prey-species

populations that support them, and about the management of habitats intended to provide space for them as endangered carnivores.

Impala

Northern Botswana, and especially the Okavango Delta region, provides ideal habitat for wild dogs: a mosaic of woodland patches mixed with seasonally flooded grasslands that support healthy populations of impala, red lechwe, reedbuck and kudu. Throughout most of this region impala is the predominant antelope species; we have recorded average densities that vary between three and 15 impala per square

Opposite. *A cheetah is momentarily distracted by the photographer as it stalks across an open flood plain.*

Above. *Hunting in the Okavango swamps often stops abruptly when the prey charges across a water channel that is likely to harbour crocodiles. For predator and prey alike, the decision to jump in the water is a matter of weighing the risks.*

Above. *A typical herd of impala looks alert, with dozens of pairs of eyes maintaining a high level of vigilance for predators.*

Left. *Heads up while running to follow the chase, these trailers play a part when the prey attempts to evade the closest dog by circling back.*

Opposite. *Keeping a lookout for hyenas and lions, a cheetah quickly feeds on its kill. The cheetah, a diurnal predator of medium-sized antelope, is the feline version of the wild dog. Cheetahs also share with wild dogs the unfortunate consequences of their predatory nature: persecution by ranchers.*

kilometre over a considerable portion of the driest parts of the delta, with the number depending on the habitat type. Densities are significantly higher in the woodland edge than in relatively open, flood-plain habitat: in areas with more regularly flooded grasslands interdigitating through woodland 'islands', as is the case on the west side of Chief's Island in the Moremi Wildlife Reserve, the impala density can be three times that found in similar but drier habitats.

Impala are considered an 'edge' species because they are often found in the transitional edge between relatively open woodlands and the bordering grasslands that are the two habitats they utilise most. In this sense, impala are the perfect prey species for wild dogs: they are the perfect size and the most common species, they are not particularly fast, and they live in optimal wild dog habitat.

There is a myth about wild dogs that has been recounted to us numerous times: that antelope are so terrorised by the presence of dogs they will vacate an area for several days after a pack has passed through. We know these stories are repeated, in spite of contrary direct personal experience, because they are sensational, and also because they have been told before and are rooted in local lore. However, impala – to take the predominant prey species as an example – are resident, territorial animals, and most are closely tied to a territory for much of the year. The idea that they would suddenly abandon their territories for a few days because wild dogs come by is nonsense.

Predators, especially wild dogs, are a fundamental and inseparable feature of impala habitat. Impala social groupings, choice of habitat, and foraging and reproductive behaviour (such as synchronous birthing, which refers to the short annual period during which most calves in the population are born) have evolved over millions of years precisely in response to this kind of predation and especially, because of its frequency, predation by wild dogs.

What are the prey animals' defences against wild dogs? There are many levels on which to address this question, so it merits beginning with ground-level predator-avoidance tactics – what impala do when they are chased by wild dogs. At top speeds in open areas, a healthy impala will reliably and consistently outpace a wild dog, and most unsuccessful chases end within 500 to 600 metres of where they began, with the dogs giving up and the still-visible impala pronking like a rocking horse into the distance.

Impala also take advantage of the fact that wild dogs are visual hunters – once a dog loses sight of an impala, the chase is usually finished. Impala can lose a pursuing wild dog by running into bush and rapidly changing directions to break visual contact. However, this tactic sometimes fails because the impala are forced to slow down in thick bush.

Another notable tactic has a success rate that depends on the frequency of its occurrence. A few adults or, more commonly, a few juveniles from an impala group will occasionally, depending on the vegetation, opt to hide by standing perfectly still instead of running away. We have seen this escape tactic succeed countless times, as dogs run right past stationary impala – but only because they are focused on chasing ones that are more conspicuous because they are running away. This

tactic is described as 'frequency dependent' because it can be successful only if the majority of the impala in the group continue to run away conspicuously. It is not uncommon for the impala, as soon as they consider themselves out of danger – sometimes only minutes after the dogs have run by – to quietly move a short distance away and resume browsing.

A Natural History of Predation

Responses to wild dog predation from an evolutionary perspective are complex but are essential to understanding the general features of ungulate behavioural ecology. The most conspicuous characteristic of impala natural history is that they are exceptionally social animals and are rarely seen alone. The consistent social organisation of impala into large groups (seldom fewer than twenty individuals) is not an arbitrary outcome of history or impala predisposition, but rather a solution in an adaptive and evolutionary sense to millions of years of being confronted with predictable and regular challenges in life.

Group living is interesting because there are several probable costs to individuals that live in a

group: the cost of increased competition for locally available food among the group members; that of an increased risk of disease resulting from constant close contact with others; and, because groups are more conspicuous than solitary individuals, the cost of an increased risk of being the target of any one of the numerous predators that eat them. Why, then, do impala so consistently live in large herds?

The theory that living in a group is beneficial in terms of feeding is related to the fact that for some animals food is found only in extremely

Opposite. *Predators are a constant feature of antelope habitat. Here, a male lion strolls across a flood plain grazed short by lechwe; the lechwe keep a watchful eye on the lion from a safe distance.*
Left. *The evening light through a cloud of dust softens the sharpness of what often appears a harsh natural world. Safety in numbers allows lechwe of various ages to minimise risk and still look for grass to graze, as the herd's male stands sentry at the edge of the group.*
Below. *Alert and constantly attentive, a wild dog listens for the alarm calls of the numerous social bird species and the various species of group-living antelope that keep an eye out during the middle of the day while wild dogs are normally resting.*

rich clumps or patches, for example, fruit-bearing trees in a mixed-species woodland. Patchy distribution can refer to patchiness in either space or time, and because these patches may be difficult to find it helps to have several individuals in a group looking for them, as, for example, with bees from a hive.

However, impala are considered generalist grazers and browsers. They graze in grasslands when grasses are reasonably palatable and can switch to browsing if grasses are burned or are otherwise unpalatable. It seems unlikely that impala gain any advantage from being in a herd strictly in terms of access to these foods. It is reasonable, rather, to assume that if there is any consequence of group foraging for impala, it is that it may slightly increase local food competition.

However, there are at least three potential general benefits from group living that probably outweigh these costs. These are widely applicable to all group-living animals, from insects to fish, birds and mammals, and are related to avoiding being eaten by a predator. These benefits are an increased chance of detecting predators through

greater vigilance, a decreased probability of any one individual's being captured, and an increased chance of a possible escape related to confusion.

Increased vigilance as a consequence of being in a group can benefit all the group's members in varying ways. Whether a predator is waiting in ambush or approaching openly from a distance, escape depends heavily on how soon it is detected. Being in a group increases the number of eyes looking out for danger, and only one individual need spot a threat for all the others to be alerted. More area can be scanned reliably and with greater frequency by a collection of individuals than by any one individual and, above a certain group size, a group can be optimally vigilant and still require less time from each individual than if the individual were alone. This allows group-living individuals more time to devote to other activities, such as feeding, simply as a result of being in the group.

The theory that being in a group lowers the probability of being captured, called the 'dilution effect', is based on the idea that a predator can capture only a single individual at a time. In a group of two, therefore, an individual has a fifty per cent chance of being the one to be captured, but in a group of fifty the chance, without considering any other factors, is decreased to one in fifty. (Dilution is the principle that accounts for the synchronous birthing of many of the African ungulates, including impala in the Okavango.)

There are other factors that can further affect an individual's probability of capture, such as its position in the group, and the relative age and condition of the other group members, but the simple mathematical relationship between increasing numbers and decreasing probability of being captured is sufficiently compelling to apply it to impala and African wild dogs.

Opposite. *A pup yawns as if bored with the same scenery, unaware that its life will become exciting soon enough. An average of only three out of ten pups survive through the first year.*

Above. *The success of large packs, such as this one emerging from the woodlands, is dependent on high densities of prey animals, but also on their ability to avoid predation by lions through greater vigilance.*

Right. *Lions are unpredictable in their distribution, occcurring almost anywhere in the region.*

Predators may be thwarted during a chase by the confusion generated by the large number and multiple directions of the fleeing individuals of a group. Although the effect on the success of a predator of this confusion is not well established for many species, it is often used as an evolutionary explanation for predator-avoidance behaviour in fishes and some herding animals such as zebra.

Wild dogs chasing impala are occasionally distracted by other fleeing individuals; we have seen young dogs leave off chasing one impala and start chasing another without skipping a step, and the only apparent explanation is the distraction caused to the dog by there being several impala running around in the same area. In these cases the dogs typically come away from the hunt without success. The effect of confusion on the success of African wild dogs chasing impala is

questionable, but we cannot dismiss it as a possible benefit of living in a large group.

The evolutionary solutions to the constant pressure of predators are as varied as the species that fall into the category of potential prey for wild dogs. Reedbuck live primarily in monogamous pairs and use the cover of tall grasses for escape. Kudu are associated more with woodland habitats and occur typically in small groups of five to seven; their large size and cryptic coloration provide them with some measure of safety from the usual assortment of predators, and in Botswana only juveniles and subadult kudu are subject to predation pressure by wild dogs.

Red lechwe are sturdy antelope, about half again the size of impala, but are associated strictly with wetland, flooded grassland and swamp habitats – lechwe rely entirely on the wide, flat stretches of flood-plain water for their escape

Opposite, below. *Because of its hunting frequency and efficiency,* Lycaon *probably has had the most profound impact of all the predators on shaping the behaviour and ecology of medium-sized antelope.*

Opposite, above; right and below right. *In the fading evening light an adult male impala, tripped up in marshy ground after a long chase, falls prey to a pack of wild dogs. Death follows quickly as the dogs tear open the belly just behind the ribs and, with seemingly surgical precision, snip out the heart and lungs in a matter of seconds. A faster method to dispatch their antelope prey would be difficult to imagine.*

from pursuing predators. They occur in very high densities in some habitats and therefore would provide a substantial resource for any predator able to work out a reliable way of capturing them.

Because red lechwe regularly graze on the grasses that grow on the dry land at the edge of flood waters, African wild dogs in the Okavango Delta and in other flooded habitats consider them the next-best thing to impala, and some packs of dogs become quite adept at capturing these antelope, even in water.

The water of the Okavango presents more than just an obstacle for wild dogs to overcome in the pursuit of lechwe. Water represents a profound risk to wild dogs because it conceals untold numbers of crocodiles, one of the few predators that eats wild dogs. At the edge of the water, crocodiles can turn the tables on wild dogs, which go suddenly from being predators to being potential prey.

The importance of crocodiles in the behaviour of dogs can be observed any time a pack approaches a body of water: extreme caution and excessive anxiety characterise the behaviour of wild dogs as they approach water to get a hasty

Above left. *After a chase, the pack regroups and waits anxiously for the hunters to return.*
Left. *Not deep enough to hide a crocodile, the smooth surface of a rainwater pan reflects a painted dog.*
Above. *As with many of the bovid species, buffalo are regularly found in large herds which afford some protection from the larger predators such as lions and hyenas.*

Wild Dogs as Prey

drink or survey it for a crossing. Even this caution, complete with alarm growls at anything looking remotely suspicious in the water, is occasionally insufficient, as a lightning-speed lunge by a crocodile snaps a dog off its heels and yanks it instantly under the water, never to be seen again. From our point of view, wild dogs that are taken by predators simply disappear – unless we actually see the predation event we have no way of knowing what has happened to the numerous individuals that just vanish.

Crocodiles are not the most significant predators of wild dogs. Lions and hyenas also constitute an ever-present threat, and lions alone probably represent the single most important natural cause of mortality in healthy populations of wild dogs. Lions often go out of their way to aggressively pursue wild dogs, irrespective of whether the lions are hungry or whether they have young cubs to protect. In fact, when lions do

succeed in killing a wild dog, they rarely eat it, and have been recorded doing so only when they are old, alone or extremely hungry.

Although the aggression directed at African wild dogs by lions has casually been explained as an attempt to eliminate a competitor, evidence suggests that wild dogs compete only slightly in terms of prey-species overlap with lions. Furthermore, wild dogs regularly provide for lions by making kills that lions immediately and easily appropriate. Lions seem to maintain this

predator-prey relationship with wild dogs based on an enmity out of all proportion with the costs and benefits of their aggression and the impact wild dogs have on their lives. Wild dogs have evolved through millions of years of predation pressure from lions. Therefore, our understanding of wild dog social behaviour and ecology might be advanced by incorporating the ever-present risk of their being killed as prey.

Earlier in this chapter, two fundamental explanations for group living in animals were identified: to enhance feeding and to avoid predation. In the past, speculation about the ultimate function of group living for African wild dogs has focused predominantly on the hypothesis that living in packs enables wild dogs to capture large prey – the 'enhanced food' hypo-

thesis. We now know, though, that African wild dogs often capture impala, their most common and, in this sense, 'preferred' prey, single-handed (see Chapter Three).

We have also seen several packs of wild dogs start with only a single pair of adults, a mating system that differs from the normal co-operative pack system of wild dogs but is typical of other canids such as side-striped jackals (*Canis adustus*) and bat-eared foxes (*Otocyon megalotis*). Several of these pairs of wild dogs successfully whelped a litter of pups while provisioning them from their impala kills in exactly the same way that a larger pack does.

However, all but one of these small packs eventually failed, not because the pair could not feed the pups but because either the adults or the

pups were killed by lions before the pups reached an age where they could contribute as adults to their own and their parents' protection. In one pair the male was killed while the female was still pregnant; she abandoned the pups and eventually died alone, of unknown causes. In another, the mother was killed by lions before the pups were weaned. In a third, the majority of the pups had already been killed before the age of four months, and the mother was also killed by a lion while she was feeding from an impala kill.

The fact that African wild dogs commonly fall prey to lions has caused us to consider the alternative hypothesis – that wild dogs live in packs primarily in response to intense lion preda-tion pressure – and we have found considerable evidence in support of this hypothesis.

Opposite, above. *With the enthusiasm and determination to carry them over their normal apprehension of deep water, these dogs persist with the capture of a male lechwe into a deep channel while hoping for help from the trailing pack.*
Opposite, below. *An adult stalks in the open, with ears flat and head held low, to close the distance between it and its intended prey.*
Above. *Cheetah use their vice-like jaws to strangle their prey, then drag it quietly out of sight to eat as much as possible. If discovered by lions, spotted hyenas or wild dogs, they leave the remains and run.*

Above. *Eye contact bridges the abyss between life and death as if to illustrate the fundamental relationship between the two – the death of the lechwe simultaneously means survival for the dogs. There is nothing as certain as death, a part of the natural, constantly self-renewing process of life.*

Living in a pack alleviates the extreme consequences of predation pressure – total pack failure – in at least two ways. The benefits of group living described earlier for ungulate prey species apply equally to wild dogs and their relationship with lions. Increased vigilance is an extremely important function of pack living, and this can be observed at any kill where multiple age groups are present. Older wild dogs in the pack, which are excluded from eating until the younger ones have

finished (see Chapter Three), fan out from the carcass and watch out for lions and hyenas. Hyenas are readily chased away but if an approaching lion is sighted the sentries sound an alarm to which all the dogs immediately respond. In many cases the lions simply remain with the pirated carcass while the dogs protest with alarm barks from a safe distance, but it is not uncommon for some of the lions to make a concerted effort to kill some of the dogs before settling in with the appropriated kill.

Wild dogs can more effectively avoid predation by lions by being in a group as a result of the increased probability of detecting a predator – more dogs mean more eyes available for vigilance. Although there are no specialists that assume sentry duty in a pack, we have found that pack vigilance increases proportionally with pack size. All dogs, unless physically compromised (with an injury or illness), are constantly attentive to noises and activities around them, even when they are resting.

The wild dog pack also provides an important buffer against predation by the principle of dilution, described previously for herds of impala. If lions succeed in ambushing a wild dog pack, usually only a single dog is killed. From the perspective of any individual in the pack, the probability of its being the one captured decreases the more members there are in the group. From the perspective of an average wild dog pack and its collective reproductive success, the loss of a single

Top. *With its back to the water, a cowed spotted hyena tries to fend off the wild dogs' aggressive, sharp teeth.*
Above. *A nose hold is commonly known by livestock handlers to subdue almost any animal. Wild dogs appear to be well apprised of this tactic and use it effectively to control the sharp horns of adult antelope.*

Above. *Teamwork enables wild dogs to rend their prey into pieces in just seconds after the pack assembles at a kill. Here, the dogs' pulling against each other on the last of the carcass helps tear away the skin from the few edible remains.*

individual does not usually translate into total reproductive failure, as it usually does for just a pair of wild dogs.

The concept of African wild dogs as prey animals is counter to the general image of them as daring and indefatigable carnivores; it requires a shift in our perspective. Wild dogs are subject to predation pressures in the same way as the animals on which they make their living, though,

and, as with all species in the food-chain continuum, they too have evolved avoidance behaviours and social organisation in response to that predation. Only when we appreciate this rich and broad context of relationships between species and the long history of co-evolution between all predators and their prey can we fully understand the complex patterns of animal behaviour and social organisation.

Above right. *Tall grass after the rains makes cursorial hunting more difficult for wild dogs, which bound as if on springs in order to try to maintain visual contact with more agile, longer-legged prey.*

Pressure

Wildlife conservation is first and foremost

an issue about land and the natural resources associated with it.

Northern Botswana hosts approximately 700 to 800 wild dogs, one of only three populations containing more than an estimated 250 to 300 dogs in the whole of Africa. Although Botswana's population currently appears to be a robust one with a wide distribution, its survival into the next century is by no means assured. Because there is typically only one breeding pair in an average pack, fewer than 100 pairs constitute the entire breeding population for the species in Botswana. In this light, the various pressures that threaten the future of Botswana's wildlife and wilderness areas are magnified in relation to their effects on wild dogs.

The pressures that bear directly on the survival of wildlife species such as African wild dogs can broadly be attributed to a slow but continuous loss of wilderness habitats. As competition for resources increases with a rapidly growing human population, the frequency of conflict with livestock escalates, resulting in damaging perceptions and the persecution of wildlife, while at the same time the threat of domestic-animal diseases becomes ever more pronounced.

These growing pains in northern Botswana are similar to problems that exist in developing countries elsewhere in the world, but Botswana has its own unique and interesting characteristics and turns of history which are essential components of any and all potential solutions. Government decision makers, local citizens and international tourists all have an interest and a role to play in the future of northern Botswana and the spectacular natural resources of the Okavango Delta. By default, all have become the stewards of one of Africa's last remaining wilderness areas.

To understand the pressures that are squeezing the wildlife of Botswana into increasingly confined spaces, the political and cultural history of Botswana, a handful of key historical events and the economic significance of the commercial cattle industry have to be taken into account.

The Botswana Cattle Story

Previous page, left. *Fresh water is arguably the most precious natural resource in southern Africa, and the Okavango – 15 000 square kilometres of wetland Eden in a sea of Kalahari sand – is a wealth of what every living thing requires.*
Previous page, right. *The dominant female cleans out her den. The tyre tracks from tourist vehicles, behind the dog, illustrate the impact of well-intentioned human presence.*
Above. *Unperturbed by the radio collar, a yearling pulls at the remains of an impala. Although it would be preferable to avoid using radiotelemetry,*

it is the only effective method of consistently and reliably monitoring free-ranging wild dogs.
Above right. *A herd of zebra grazes in the resource-rich Okavango, in cattle-free habitats reserved for wildlife management and utilisation. In a growing population with growing livestock herds, these grasslands are coveted resources.*
Opposite, below. *Unlike most wild large canids, wild dogs are tolerant of human presence and provide rewarding opportunities for wildlife and photographic tourism. In a land of sharp contrasts, this tolerance is not without a cost, however.*

It was late afternoon. A dusty, blue-grey wind swept by the open windows of our vehicle as Kenneth Molepo, my research assistant, and I raced the setting sun on our way home. We had spent a long day in the village, conducting interviews with the local residents regarding the conflict between livestock and wildlife. Our hitchhiker in the back seat was putting on his jacket, his cattle post just ahead.

Suddenly a pack of five wild dogs crossed the road right in front of us. I thought I recognised one from its unusual golden-yellow colour, and I noticed that the dogs looked in good condition. Were they hunting? Why here? My heart raced. On the road, well beyond the protected-area boundaries, amid people and cattle posts – this was dangerous territory for wild dogs.

The dogs quickly disappeared into the mopane scrub at the side of the road. I hesitated, anxious to follow, to determine which dogs they were and if one was wearing a radio collar. Before I had a chance to move, however, three young calves barrelled out of the mopane and the loud bawling of a dying calf sounded like an air horn from behind them. 'Those are my cows!' shouted the hitchhiker, jumping out of the vehicle and dashing into the bush. We followed. Only 40 metres in from the road, standing over a dead calf, was the hitchhiker and his brother. 'I'll kill them! Horrible creatures – if I had a gun, I would shoot all those dogs!' the brother declared, furious.

The dogs had already left, and there was nothing to do but carry the calf back to the cattle post for butchering. Kenneth and I drove off in silence. I felt sick. The cattle were attended by a herder, and were being taken to the kraal for the night – the kind of responsible livestock care which we thought would eliminate depredation problems. Is it possible, I wondered, for people and wildlife to share the same space?

Journal notes, LPB, 19 July 1995.

The original inhabitants of the Kalahari desert and the Okavango Delta were the click-speaking Basarwa (also known as San or Khoi San), traditional hunter-gatherers who have been in the region for over 10 000 years. The Tswana, who have an agropastoral history dating back to AD 400, are currently Botswana's largest and politically dominant ethnic group. Their pastoralist culture, supported by British protectorate initiatives, has dominated the economic and political development of the country.

Traditionally, pastoralists and their livestock nomadically followed seasonal rains, just as wildlife had done for thousands of years before

them. The general scarcity of water kept herd sizes low and grazing of grasslands to a sustainable level, while the traditional response to limited grazing was simply to move to a new area, as space was, to all intents and purposes, limitless. A rapidly growing human population and, especially, the development of a new commercial cattle industry in Botswana have changed this nomadic lifestyle, and still contribute today to changing the face of the nation's environment.

In a global climate of modernisation based on rapid development and growth, the protectorate government began initiatives in the 1930s to develop the commercial cattle industry in Botswana. Developing a disease-free cattle industry turned out to be logistically challenging, however, and required the exploitation of the two politically most sensitive resources, water and land. It also resulted in the erection of hundreds of kilometres of veterinary cordon fences for

Above. *A large pack of dogs stalks across a wide-open Okavango flood plain – a slow prelude to a high-speed chase. Wild dogs require extensive wildlife habitats in which to range, but expansive wild habitats are under continuously increasing pressure from growing human-population needs. Loss of habitat is one of several reasons for the decline in the wild dog population.*

Right. *Quenching its thirst, an adult drinks from clear, shallow waters – liquid gold in a parched desert environment.*
Below right. *Perceptions of wild dogs as dangerous or threatening to people are unfounded. We have never heard an account, credible or otherwise, of a wild dog attacking a human.*

quarantine purposes, an enormous investment in the creation of artificial waterholes and efforts to control the disease-carrying tsetse fly in the Okavango Delta.

These developments increased the pressure on natural resources, especially those in northern Botswana and the Okavango Delta, a wildlife-rich wetland ecosystem nestled in the heart of an otherwise inhospitable desert. Developments opened previously uninhabitable areas for live-stock grazing, which, by default, had hitherto been the reserve of Botswana's wildlife.

Perhaps as a legacy of colonial involvement in Botswana's developing cattle industry, the European Economic Community (EEC), now known as the European Union (EU), has sub-sidised Botswana's beef industry since the early 1970s. These EU subsidies guarantee an export market for Botswana's beef industry at rates often well above European market prices. This agree-ment not only subsidises beef exports in Botswana, it also helps to provide financing for commercial livestock operations in the form of boreholes, ranch leases and stock acquisitions.

Critics of the subsidy believe that Botswana's semi-arid desert environment cannot sustain large-scale commercial cattle ranching and that artificial support for the cattle industry only establishes incentives that virtually ensure envi-ronmental degradation. They also point out that most subsidy benefits go directly to the relatively few owners of Botswana's large cattle operations, thereby arguably defeating the overall objectives of international development assistance.

Few would argue, however, that the beef sub-sidies have helped to create a substantial com-mercial cattle industry in Botswana where one previously did not exist.

The veterinary cordon fences which criss-cross Botswana, partitioning the country into large blocks intended to control the movements of animals, were the direct result of the colonial support that continued in Botswana after the country's independence. The beef subsidy agreement, which stipulated compliance with international quarantine regulations to control foot-and-mouth disease, resulted in the erection of hundreds of kilometres of fences, known locally as buffalo fences. These fences served primarily to physically separate wildlife from domestic stock. In accomplishing this, the fences have impacted dramatically on the movement – and consequently the survival – of many of Botswana's wildlife populations. They also have limited the mobility of people and their cattle, forcing a change from traditionally nomadic, pastoral lifestyles to more spatially concentrated, relatively sedentary pastoralist practices. In this sense, the fences have been instrumental in preventing cattle from entering the last remaining wildlife-management areas, and it has been argued that without them perhaps no wildlife areas would now exist free of cattle.

Q: What are your thoughts about the buffalo fence?

A: Before the buffalo fence, there was lots of game. After the fence, there was so much less. There used to be free movement of animals and there were many animals; now the border keeps them away and there are more cattle posts.

The buffalo fence should be extended to where the cattle posts are so the livestock can't go as far away and cannot meet the predators.

Interview, LPB, 2 August 1995.

Second to cordon fences, the main investment in Botswana's commercial cattle industry has been in the development of artificial water points. Each successful borehole allows areas previously unsuitable for livestock because of a lack of water to be exploited as grazing land. By the time of independence in 1966, more than 1 000 boreholes had already been drilled, and countless more have been drilled in the past 30 years. Drilling boreholes in Botswana has become common practice, continuously expanding the amount of land suitable for cattle and people, at the expense of land previously used only by wildlife.

Borehole development also contributed importantly to changes in traditional patterns of rural land use by introducing private ownership of water as a resource. This change in resource ownership began a long process of redefining

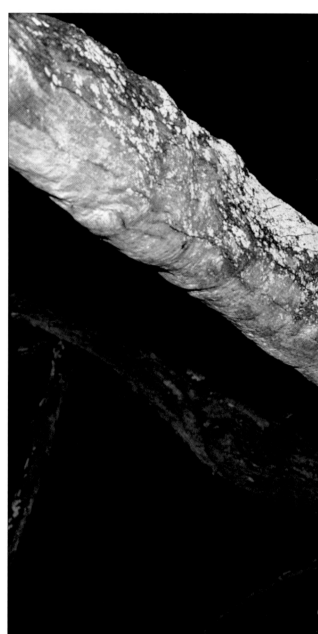

Left. *An aerial view of a cattle post. The surroundings are typically devoid of any ground-cover vegetation, a condition that expands from the cattle posts as the dry season progresses. Government policies have attempted to privatise, enclose and regulate the livestock business in the hopes of reducing overgrazing.*

rights of access to resources and land-tenure laws that continues to shape the ways in which natural resources are utilised in Botswana today.

Since the early 1800s human settlement patterns in the resource-rich Okavango Delta region have been determined by two key factors: the distribution of water and diseases. Mosquito-borne malaria is widespread throughout the delta, but the tsetse fly had the greatest influence on the pattern of human settlement and activity in the delta owing to the disease it carries, trypanosomiasis, which afflicts cattle (in humans it is known as sleeping sickness). Efforts over the last two

decades to completely eradicate tsetse fly with spraying and chemical trapping have failed, but the fly's distribution has successfully been reduced and current controls are in place to keep it that way – a success that has contributed to the continuing development of northern Botswana as suitable rangeland for domestic stock.

Changes that have led to the claiming of previously unsuitable wilderness areas for livestock represent the underlying causes of habitat fragmentation and loss, the primary reason for the threatened status of many of Africa's wildlife species, especially wild dogs. For 20 years

Above. *A leopard has lifted its kill into the safety of a tall tree. Leopards, dependent on the resources of the ecosystem, are coming into conflict with increasing frequency with small livestock.*

Botswana's booming economy and democratic government have been internationally acclaimed as 'the African success story'. The cost of rapid development on Botswana's environment has put dramatic pressure on the government of Botswana to implement aggressive management of its scarce and diminishing natural resources.

Management: Balancing Cattle, People and Wildlife

Growing human and cattle populations squeezing in around the delta require access to critical resources, especially water. It is no surprise, therefore, that they look beyond the fences that separate them from the wildlife areas and flood plains of the Okavango, where the wild dog and dozens of other wildlife species persist, silently dependent on the limited resources of the Okavango ecosystem.

Range degradation was already a severe problem at the time of independence, and the cattle population, now estimated conservatively at three million, has tripled since the introduction of borehole drilling in the 1930s. Similarly, the human population of Botswana has more than doubled, to 1,8 million, since independence. In general, conditions are primed for generating extreme pressures on Botswana's natural resources and wildlife.

> Q: Are cattle important to you?
> A: Livestock is very important to us now. In times of shortage of rain, we cannot grow crops so we must keep livestock.
> *Interview, LPB, 12 August 1995.*

In recent years Botswana has taken important steps towards improving environmental and wildlife-management policy. As the human

population grows, political pressure on the government mounts to reallocate ever more wildlife areas to grazing. Recent policy changes have aimed at striking a balance between natural-resource management and satisfying the needs of the expanding human population.

Over the past 30 years Botswana has designated 36 per cent of its land to wildlife management and protection. This is divided between National Parks, Wildlife Management Areas (WMAs) and Controlled Hunting Areas (CHAs). Although Botswana resisted co-signing foreign-initiated treaties or conventions that proposed to monitor biologically diverse areas such as the Okavango Delta, the figure of 36 per cent of the country reserved for natural resources, especially wildlife, is an impressive one. Foreign donors, encouraged by this commitment, have responded generously with aid money for the management of Botswana's natural resources.

In 1986 the Wildlife Conservation Policy was proposed to promote the proper utilisation of wildlife resources through rural development and citizen participation. The policy delineated

Opposite, top. *Fire is a natural part of the ecology of northern Botswana, but increased frequency of fires caused by human activities may cause extensive damage to both wildlife and vegetation.*
Opposite, below. *Potential for conflict with livestock is entirely predictable, given the fact that wild dogs occasionally find buffalo calves suitable prey.*
Above. *More than any other species, buffalo may be responsible for the fact that wildlife areas have remained cattle-free.*

Above. *Lechwe have adapted to exploit the inundated regions of the delta where most other antelope cannot.*
Right. *Uncertain and slightly nervous, wild dogs splash through the waters of a recently flooded area, keeping a wary eye out for crocodiles.*

Opposite, below. *Lionesses, wading through shallow water in the early hours of dawn, belie the general thought that lions are averse to getting wet. Certainly, this perception of lions does not hold true in the Okavango Delta, where lions regularly cross flooded plains.*

WMAs adjoining national parks and game reserves and stipulated that they be cattle free but open to resource utilisation, such as for grass cutting and the collection of firewood, by local communities. WMAs were intended to serve as buffer zones and corridors for migratory wildlife and to provide local rural people with a sustainable resource base that included wildlife utilisation. CHAs were designed to improve the administration and control of hunting in the region through community participation in wildlife management and direct community benefit.

It seems clear that Botswana's government has consistently demonstrated legislative commitment to the long-term management of its wildlife. However, competing agendas and inadequate resources committed to the enforcement of legislation established to protect its natural resources from illegal exploitation have been a general downfall.

Since the introduction of boreholes to the dry sands underlying most of Botswana, through independence and to the present, Botswana has been in a constant process of transformation. The country began with a small mix of distinct cultures, most of which were partially nomadic and which were characterised largely by communal ownership of land and direct governance. This has been transformed into a nation that emphasises private resource ownership, central government control and economics dictated by market forces. It has been a transition by a series of legislation and policy changes that have attempted to balance culture, politics and policy. The underlying motivations appear to have been based on genuine attempts to achieve a reasonable balance for everyone, and understanding these motivations is seldom more complicated than a broad cost-benefit analysis. However, like everywhere in the world today, limited resources and competing interests make striking a satisfactory balance a nearly impossible task.

Cattle as a source of revenue and not just as a form of cultural wealth have been promoted by the government of Botswana. Market incentives encourage all citizens to acquire cattle and, like any other financially driven industry, the participants often seem unimpressed with the fact that unlimited growth of herds comes at an expense. As the number of cattle posts increases, habitats that previously supported far more productive populations (in terms of biomass) of Botswana's wildlife decline. Disregard for this stems from the fact that wildlife is chiefly a competitor for cattle.

Therefore, a diminishing wildlife population is not only a consequence of cattle farming, it is a goal.

Q: Do you like wild dogs?
    A: We would like to save wild dogs, but when they kill our cattle we have to try to shoot them. I understand they are an important part of the wildlife, but my cattle are important to my family and me for our survival.

Interview, LPB, 24 August 1995.

One of the primary problems in balancing wildlife and cattle development has been the rules

Above. *A group of pups and adults stops for a drink from a rain-filled pool before finding a place to spend the night. Small rainwater pans are sometimes too muddy from heavy elephant use to do anything but cool the feet in the soft mud.*

Left. *An unusually relaxed and unconcerned leopard is indicative of repeated contact with vehicles. Normally highly secretive, leopards adapt to relatively close proximity with people partly because they take advantage of a broad range of prey species.*

Opposite. *As the last rays of sunlight disappear behind the palms, wild dogs start the evening hunt, oblivious of the pressures facing the resource-rich ecosystem on which they depend.*

governing access to land. Traditionally, under Tswana customary law, the vast majority of suitable land was classified as communal grazing land, which meant essentially that any herder could use any rangeland. There were and are, however, no restrictions on herd size, and the solution to the problem of lack of grazing land has been to develop more grazing land by drilling more boreholes.

Motivated partly by the belief that communal land was doomed to be degraded by overgrazing, the government has made various attempts to reduce the impact of overstocking by privatising, enclosing and otherwise controlling the livestock industry. However, legislation and government policies aimed at dealing with rural community livestock management, such as drought-relief programmes, have been overwhelmingly ineffectual and overgrazing continues to be a concern today.

In the early development phase of the commercial cattle industry some land was set aside as 'freehold', a private lease of the land with which came exclusive rights. Freeholds were generally awarded to large cattle ranchers, on the understanding that this would improve range management. However, the law did not remove the rights of the larger cattle owners to also utilise communal grazing lands, thus enabling commercial ranchers to shuttle their livestock between the two, thereby gaining access to the best of both. This practice placed tremendous pressure on communal grazing lands and strongly favoured the few large commercial ranchers over the vast majority of small stock owners, and simultaneously defeated the original policy objectives.

These early reversals for smallholders have begun to be addressed by the recent policy

changes with regard to WMAs and greater community involvement in wildlife management. These policies will aim to move natural-resource decision making towards the local level, where it is less susceptible to errors of overly broad policies. Striking a balance between wildlife and livestock will still be difficult, however. While development issues and environment issues are more strongly linked at the community level, there are still strong pressures favouring cattle production. The difficult balance between wildlife and cattle remains more a goal for the future than a present reality.

Management of wildlife and wild dogs in Botswana has taken place in the cultural context of widespread reverence for cattle and the social context of a multiplicity of cultures with differing traditions of wildlife use. Overlaid on these

cultural factors have been the forces of economic development similar to those faced in all countries. In the past in Botswana, as in most developed and developing countries, environmental and especially wildlife issues have taken a back seat to economic growth. Development has been based at least in part on a few widely held but not necessarily correct assumptions that relate to environmental circumstances. These are, firstly, that the environment has an infinite capacity for self-renewal; secondly, that human population growth is not a problem; and, thirdly, that modernisation and mechanisation are unquestionably the appropriate roads to development.

Botswana, along with the rest of the world, is now beginning to question these assumptions, and management reflecting a new and deeper understanding of the environment and which is essential to establishing the necessary balance of natural-resource utilisation and economic growth is emerging.

Other Pressures: Natural and Mythical

Cattle and politics constitute the background on which the future survival and management of African wild dogs depends. However, other dynamics, including natural factors such as drought, geology and long-term changes in climate, have brought humans and wild dogs closer together, and the negative attitudes regarding wild dogs have not improved with this increased contact.

Water, the key to survival of most species, is an increasingly limited resource in northern Botswana. A hundred years ago the pristine waters of the Okavango flowed with abandon, annually flooding the river banks to cover thousands of square kilometres of thirsty land, and travelling hundreds of kilometres to eventually seep into the Kalahari. The region has experienced a general drying of the flooded areas and the gradual shifting of rivers from one side of the delta to another.

The primary factor bringing people and wild dogs closer together is the shrinking availability of surface water. Although not fully understood, it is generally accepted that faulting associated with earthquake activity plays an important part in altering the flow of water within the delta. Whatever the cause, there is less water today than there was 50 years ago, as rivers such as the Okavango and Chobe, once perennial, have become partially or wholly seasonal. As surface water shrinks and the people dependent on its resources converge in increasing numbers around the periphery of the delta, the frequency of human conflict with wild carnivores is guaranteed to increase.

There is no doubt that African wild dogs continue to suffer from a poor public image and would benefit from a public-relations ambassador. Persecution by man is probably the most disturbing pressure facing the wild dog – disturbing because persecution is often linked to negative attitudes, and most negative attitudes and images connected with the wild dog are unfounded. Human reactions to predators are often strongly and deeply emotional, and emotions commonly shape our attitudes. As a general rule, African wild dogs are thought to be dangerous, vicious and, ultimately, simply a problem.

Local attitudes in Botswana concerning African wild dogs are analogous with local attitudes concerning wolves in North America. Many North American cattle farmers, few of whom have ever personally seen a wolf, harbour an impassioned hostility towards these canids. Reputation alone, nurtured by folklore and rumour, is evidently sufficient to cause a profound distaste for an animal. It is interesting and real human behaviour, but it cannot be considered rational.

We have investigated the origins of attitudes and fears about African wild dogs in northern Botswana and found a similar pattern. In July 1995, personal interviews were conducted in four

Opposite, above. *A pup, begging a returning hunter to regurgitate, illustrates the near-perpetual mouth-to-mouth contact of wild dogs that makes them more susceptible as a group to infectious diseases.*

Opposite, below. *It is easy to see why humans tend to project their understanding from close contact with domestic dogs ('man's best friend') on to wild dogs, especially pups. It is ironic, therefore, that persecution by man has been a primary cause of wild dog mortality.*

Above. *An elephant cow lifts its trunk to pick up a scent. Another endangered species dependent on wildlife areas in Botswana, elephants are unknowing allies of wild dogs in their ongoing struggle against diminishing habitats and increasing conflict.*

Left. *Blood from a kill dries and falls out of the matted hair in just a few hours. Although wild dogs are often perceived as being perpetually dirty, they actually remain remarkably clean, and the general health of the Botswana population has been good during the recent past.*

Opposite, above. *A nearly universal sight in most of Botswana outside the buffalo fences, cattle meander along a rural calcrete road. For many of Botswana's citizens wealth lies in cattle ownership, and wildlife is regarded as competition.*

Opposite, below. *From the air, the steady encroachment of human population and livestock on the boundaries of the Okavango Delta is clearly visible. Conservatively estimated at three million, the country's cattle population has tripled since the 1930s.*

local villages in the Santawane area, bordering the Moremi Wildlife Reserve. Of the 70 local citizens interviewed, none had ever experienced personal injury or physical contact with wild dogs; none had ever heard of anyone being injured by wild dogs, and some had never seen a wild dog. A small fraction of those interviewed had direct experience with livestock loss. They all, however, expressed fear of and most expressed hostility towards wild dogs.

> Q: Have you ever heard of a case where wild dogs attacked or injured people?
> A: No, but now that the drought is coming, we must all be extra careful as wild dogs will come to attack people.
> *Interview, LPB, 22 August 1995.*

When direct experience, as opposed to myth and folklore, is involved in shaping attitudes and behaviour about wildlife, fear and finances together constitute the most relevant factors. Livestock depredation by wild carnivores is indisputably a problem for some livestock owners. At one time there was a value placed on wild dogs and they were condemned at the same time: stories of bounty hunting in what were then Rhodesia and Northern Rhodesia tell of how young hunters were paid 'good pocket money' for each wild dog tail brought in. Currently there is

no market value in the meat or skins of wild dogs, and these carnivores are perceived merely as destructive and valueless.

The impact of predation on an average livestock owner in Botswana can be devastating but, considered collectively, alleged livestock predation by wild dogs amounts to less than one per cent of the national livestock herd, far less than the estimated 16 per cent average lost annually, for example, to livestock diseases. More intense attendance and management of livestock might help significantly to reduce the loss of livestock to wild carnivores.

The Unexpected

Persecution by man, directly through hunting and poisoning, for example, has been a primary cause of wild dog population declines throughout Africa. With this in mind, it is ironic that the direct interface between wild dogs and humans through tourism might now have the single most positive influence on their conserva-

tion. Because wild dogs have suffered a near-fatal population decline throughout most of their historical range in Africa, the population in Botswana now attracts considerable attention and tourism revenue to the country. Local government acknowledgment that African wild dogs may have some value in Botswana may be considered the most significant result of their recent climb in stature.

As international travel becomes more accessible to the people of the world, the appeal and importance of low-impact ecotourism increases. In Botswana, the government has recognised the economic value of a growing tourism industry and has begun investing in its further growth and development. For the most part, increasing tourism is positive: it contributes to increasing awareness about conservation issues in the region and brings the opportunity of jobs, training and education in wildlife conservation.

However, tourism development is not without its own form of environmental cost. Developing infrastructure, such as modern roads

and an increase in vehicle traffic, already causes increasing numbers of wild dogs to be killed by vehicles every year in Botswana. In addition, frequent human contact and habituation can also jeopardise wild dog survival. Although we cannot deny the excitement of a 'close encounter' with a pack of African wild dogs, constant contact with

Above. *A typical island, set in the expanse of wetlands of the Okavango, is representative of this unique and still untrammelled wilderness. Just one of the wildlife-community members, African wild dogs have enjoyed the abundance of resources afforded by this wealth of water.*
Left. *An image of innocence and wilderness, an African wild dog pup stares into an uncertain future.*
Opposite. Lycaon pictus *is an endangered species that may be in the twilight of its existence. Only a concerted effort that identifies wildlife as an important natural resource will prevent pushing the species over the brink.*

tourist vehicles can and does result in habituation of wild dogs to people. The cost of this inadvertent spin-off from increased tourism is revealed when habituated dogs move outside of the protected areas (as many do) and find themselves in a livestock area with no wildlife prey. Wild dogs habituated to vehicles and humans invariably pay a heavy price for their contact with friendly tourists once they have crossed their protected-area boundaries, as their lack of fear of humans increases the likelihood that they will be killed by vehicles or in livestock areas.

Q: What are your thoughts on the development of tourism in the area?

A: Tourism is good and bad. It is good if it is restricted to photography because it does not take anything away and gives jobs to people and their children. It is also good for educating our people; Botswana has no zoos and our children need to learn about wildlife and its habitats.

It is bad, however, because it limits the freedom of Botswana citizens into the areas where we used to live. It also disturbs government programmes, such as the tsetse fly trapping, that are designed to help Botswana's citizens.

Interview, LPB, 21 July 1995.

History has defined the remaining habitat, the 'threatened space' available to this endangered carnivore. If this space were to remain in perpetuity and free of external pressures, we could begin to identify the precise long-term conservation needs of northern Botswana's wild dog population. Unfortunately, the area of land devoted to wilderness and the wildlife populations that it supports is declining every year in Botswana, and the daily survival of individual wild dogs is growing steadily more difficult.

Still today, land-use policies are being decided and implemented. Because these policies will impact on the remaining wildlife as a general matter of course, the long-term survival of Botswana's African wild dog population still hangs in uncertainty.

Despite man's historical persecution of this fascinating canid, as well as its vulnerability to domestic dog diseases, the steady loss of habitat from expanding cattle and human populations, which compete with wildlife for land, ultimately puts the greatest pressure on the last of the continent's painted wolves.

Prescription

Success in any conservation effort anywhere in the world,

whether directed at an endangered species or tropical forests, will depend on the

social and economic security of the people who live directly in its shadow.

The people who live in direct contact with a resource are not necessarily the people who have the most to lose by its decay. A country's natural resources constitute the basis of a nation's wealth, the heritage of all its citizens. Managed utilisation of natural resources can affect prosperity not just in terms of creating localised employment but also through a steady generation of income, including and especially foreign currencies, which affects the economic development of the entire country. Therefore, mismanagement and eventual loss of natural resources must be considered a loss for the entire nation. For this reason, natural-resource management normally and rightfully falls on the shoulders of the central government whose job it is to steer a nation's development in a responsible direction.

Although a central government may set the course for the development and utilisation of its national wealth in natural resources, those resources are typically most severely affected by the small fraction of, usually, local people who physically have access to them. Communal ownership in the broad, national sense – with central government control at one level of resource exploitation and local utilisation at another – presents a dilemma which is at the core of virtually all conservation issues in Botswana. These two levels of resource value and exploitation are not necessarily mutually exclusive, but management solutions must accommodate both if they are to be solutions in the long term.

What to do about wildlife conservation in Botswana, and specifically what to do about wild dogs? This is a question without an obvious answer. With fewer than five thousand remaining in the world, the fate of African wild dogs is dependent on an immediate and collective commitment by the global

community and the local stewards of Africa's remnant wilderness habitats. If, through unconstrained antipathy, misunderstanding or even apathy, we allow the existence of *Lycaon pictus* to slip between the cracks into extinction when it is in our power to determine its fate, then what are the chances of the multitude of other species following in the same path?

Although only a single example of the issues that must be addressed over and over again by Botswana's natural-resource managers, the question of wild dogs in Botswana identifies the difficult but central role of the government to establish some management objective. A common beginning point might be to address the question that to many of us is not actually a question: 'Is the conservation of African wild dogs important?' This question is not, of course, particular to wild dogs, or to any other endangered species; in fact, it could be asked generally of any species, including our own. We regard it as a 'non-question' because it presupposes there is more than one answer.

Previous page, left. *Shrouded in a hazy veil of dust and subdued light, a pack heads off into an uncertain future.*

Previous page, right. *Warm sunlight captures the tired gaze of a dependent and vulnerable pup.*

Opposite, above. *The migratory behaviour of buffalo has been severely restricted by the hundreds of kilometres of fences erected across the country to control foot-and-mouth disease. Buffalo herds are now being compressed into the centre of the Okavango, and fence building continues to control domestic-stock diseases.*

Opposite, below. *Disposed to cooperate, a two-year-old female with a belly full of meat stands among pups of two different ages at the edge of the den. Areas that support such successful wild dog packs are increasingly rare.*

Right. *The leopard is one of the species that, because it is considered a valuable trophy animal among game hunters, lends itself to the perception that the value of wildlife can be defined in terms of rands and cents.*

There is only one answer to those of us who believe that all living things, not only humans, have their own intrinsic value – a value that neither can be, nor needs to be, defined in terms of rands and cents – that the living things on this earth are important simply because they are here, like us, after the millions of years of life on our planet. However, while it is philosophically simple to assert that all life on earth is important, the solutions needed to mitigate conflict between wildlife and people become complex in the harsh glare of real problems.

African wild dogs are integral members of the complex interactive ecosystem in which they live. As a species they represent key players in regulating the health of the entire system. Because they range so widely in comparison to most other animals, a population of African wild dogs requires huge tracts of natural areas in which to move. African wild dogs are considered an important 'indicator species', because the fact that an area supports a healthy and successful wild dog population is a solid indication that the general state of the habitat is also healthy – an ecosystem must be supporting substantial populations of antelope in order to support a population of African wild dogs, which depend on the antelope for prey. In this sense, a sustainable future for *Lycaon pictus* in an ecosystem is the same as a sustainable future for wildlife in general.

Northern Botswana's remaining wildlife stronghold is the Okavango Delta, a wilderness area which has been recognised internationally, for example by the World Heritage Commission

of the World Conservation Union (IUCN), as one of the world's ecologically important wetlands. Rich in natural resources, the Okavango is a haven for numerous threatened wildlife species, including the majority of northern Botswana's African wild dog population. The Okavango also provides for the primarily subsistence lifestyles of the rural indigenous people of northern Botswana. These limited and diminishing resources are coming under increasing competitive pressure from an expanding human population and the developing regional economy.

In an attempt to more effectively manage its resources under increasing demand for them,

Botswana's legislation has steadily transferred greater management responsibilities to the central government. This control has fuelled an adversarial relationship between central government and the rural local people, who view the government as increasingly prohibitive with what they consider to be their rights to natural resources. At the heart of this antagonism is conflict over land use, with pastoralists and traditional hunters voicing equally their discontent.

Pastoralists rely primarily on livestock as a source of income and status. They resist policy-driven efforts to restrict grazing areas for the protection of wildlife, because they want access

Above. *The success of wild dogs depends on their having natural populations of antelope to sustain them. Here, a pack captures a male lechwe as the sun hovers on the edge of the tree line.*
Opposite, above. *Like a dog before the hearth, a wild dog lying curled up and asleep conjures up images of familiar scenes with domestic dogs.*
Opposite, below. *Seeing tracks of wild dogs is an encouraging sign that this endangered species has not vanished altogether.*

to more grazing land. Traditional hunters, some of whom are dependent on wildlife for subsistence, resist the steady reduction of their hunting allowances by government and continue to hunt. Government, in the meantime, has to walk the fine line in a political sense – keeping in mind the fact that it is a democratically elected body – between developing a regional tourist- and wildlife-based industry that is sustainable, and the cattle industry, which has been the economic and cultural foundation of the country but which may be entirely unsustainable in the near future with the rate of human population growth. Wildlife, therefore, remains in the centre

of the conflict and utterly dependent on human political decisions to allocate the resources necessary for its very existence.

Humans, because of our number, needs, resourcefulness and technologies, hold the reins of the future for the rest of the biological world. We are already in nearly constant conflict with other animals around the world over crowded habitats, and that crowding is continuously increasing as the world's human population continues to grow. Identifying the precise sources and extent of actual conflict is a prerequisite to finding acceptable compromises and real solutions for managing it, and the litmus test for

sustainable success will invariably be a change in local people's attitudes and behaviour towards wildlife. A change establishing that the managed resources are in some way directly important and valuable to local people is essential, but most critical to this is the provision of alternative resources for basic needs.

Understanding Attitudes

Cross-cultural studies worldwide have shown that there is consistently strong local public commitment to manage wildlife simply based on human values, but that utilitarian and materialistic

Above. *An old male snaps at a pesky fly. The tsetse fly in Botswana may be the wild dogs' best friend, as its persistence is the primary reason wild habitats still exist in the Okavango.*
Above right. *Two hyenas head out briskly on their nightly hunting sojourn. Hyenas are also in constant conflict with livestock in Botswana.*

goals often dominate. Idealistic views of nature and wildlife contribute to wildlife conservation, but the bottom line in human terms is necessity. In Botswana, research has shown that a pronounced utilitarian attitude towards wildlife, together with a somewhat fatalistic perception that the individual is powerless against nature to make a difference, prevents many individuals from becoming personally involved in wildlife conservation. It has been suggested that this may change,

as the combination of education, widespread depletion of animals and a growing sense of self-recrimination for the imminent loss of the cultural heritage that animals represent will eventually lead to the emergence of widespread activism.

The future remains an unknown. What is clear is that wildlife is a valuable natural resource for different reasons to different segments of society. Individuals may utilise wildlife for subsistence or commercial gain, while communities may value

wildlife for its cultural or spiritual significance, and the state may appreciate it for its broader economic potential. Understanding these differences in attitudes towards wildlife as a natural resource is fundamental to long-term conservation and management, as is realising that evaluating attitudes at all levels in terms of utilisation is difficult because they are not necessarily static or compatible. Herein lies the conservation challenge of the coming decades.

Reducing Conflict

I think it is possible to reduce conflict. I think the Department of Wildlife should come and scare the animals to the other side of the fence. That way, they cannot kill any livestock.
Interview, LPB, 27 June 1995.

Understanding that resources in the rich Okavango Delta are finite is a difficult concept to

accept or appreciate. The notion of diminishing space and the feeling of being squeezed by neighbours is clear enough to the rural people of northern Botswana, but a common perception is that the squeeze is primarily because the government has built fences, stopping the people from going farther into the delta. The most commonly suggested solution is for the wildlife (meaning the fences) to be moved farther into the delta, in order to provide more space for people and cattle.

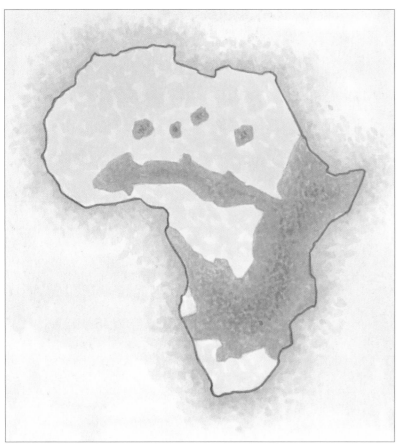

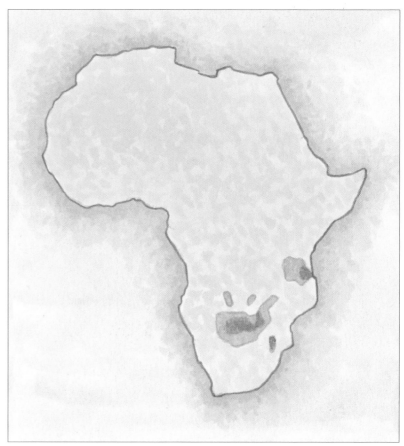

Distribution of Lycaon pictus *in Africa, 1980 (after Smithers, 1983).*

Distribution of Lycaon pictus *in Africa, 1996.*

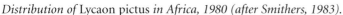

On all sides of the Okavango the rural people propose the same solutions, however – the people in the north say the same as those in the south, and the common perception is that there is unlimited space lying just on the other side of the fence. This perception can be dispelled only through education and general awareness, but until there is an understanding of the finite nature of land and the fact that resources are limited, creating an acceptance of imposed boundaries will be extremely difficult.

In the past, creating distinct boundaries to separate people from wildlife was regarded as the best conservation policy. It may be that with today's changing conditions, this policy is in need of review. As the space in which we live becomes more populated and demands for the resources grow, it will become increasingly difficult to sustain protected areas in isolation.

There may be important lessons to be learned from other countries facing similar problems of wildlife and livestock conflict and common-

property management. In many parts of East Africa, for example, tourists, wildlife, local people and livestock all share the same space and resources. The region bordering the Masai Mara Game Reserve, for instance, is utilised extensively by Maasai herdsmen attending their herds of goats and cattle. However, these areas often have higher densities of wildlife than are found inside the reserve, as the migratory wildlife populations move freely following the seasonal rains, so potential for conflict is high.

The East African conservation strategy is an attempt to compromise on both sides of the conflict, in the hope of arriving at a balance between managing sustainable wildlife populations and controlled pastoralism. In the Masai Mara region, fortified livestock bomas, all-night guards and constant attendance of cattle and goats through the day have eliminated much of the conflict between grazers and wildlife. Furthermore, a government programme assures compensation for any livestock lost to wild

Opposite. *Showing a fine array of well-used canines, this old dog yawns with fatigue. Few dogs live past the age of five years but some have been known to live to 11 in the wild. The numerous ear notches here are indicative of a long history.* **Above.** *With a glint in its eye and flies around its nose, a cheetah lies back and contentedly surveys its surroundings. The cheetah is another endangered species that depends on the sustainable management of wild habitats.*

carnivores, but only if the herder can demonstrate that prescribed conditions of husbandry, such as adequate vigilance and protection of stock at night, were met.

Although this system is purported to be slow, and Kenyan pastoralists experience significant problems with the scheme, including crowding, political disempowerment and transformation of their economic systems, the programme is worth reviewing because it is an attempt to support both wildlife and people in the same geographical space and manage wildlife-livestock conflict through local practices using local technologies.

> Men make the rules, but they don't tell the animals.
>
> *Interview, LPB, 1995.*

In Botswana, grazing conditions and animal husbandry differ significantly from those in the grassy plains of parts of East Africa. While it is believed that greater attendance of livestock would go far to decrease losses to carnivores, cattle commonly range unattended for days, and sometimes weeks, in search of grass or water. As is the case in East African countries, there is a Department of Wildlife and National Parks policy in Botswana that requires stock to be secured in a boma at night if government assistance is to be given in response to 'problem animals', but ineffective enforcement procedures contribute to the policy's often being ignored – livestock killed by predators are often those that were left ranging free at night and entirely unattended. Furthermore, greater responsibility

by livestock owners for their animals would not only help reduce losses, it would also save the lives of the countless wild carnivores that are currently shot every year as 'problem animals', especially in areas that are adjacent to protected wildlife areas.

> Wild dogs have no value to me. I can't eat them or sell their skins. They only eat my cows.
> *Interview, LPB, 24 August 1995.*

There is much debate about the best solution to managing 'problem animals'. Monetary compen-

sation can serve to dissuade livestock owners from killing predators, but at the same time it removes the sense of personal responsibility for livestock and also the sense of sharing resources between animals and people. It places on the central government the entire responsibility for wildlife which, if management is going to be sustainable, must be shared by the local communities.

Compensation also needs to be fair and expedient if it is to work. Many people who experience livestock depredation losses simply do not consider the government compensation scheme a

worthwhile option. Either it is not considered adequate compensation or the bureaucratic delay is so paralysingly slow as to discourage most farmers – or both. Many predators are therefore simply shot as a solution to the problem.

Every year we have at least one radio collar returned to us, through the Department of Wildlife, by people who have shot wild dogs in response to livestock depredation. The number shot every year in Botswana in the name of 'problem-animal control' is unknown because there is no commercial value for dead wild dogs,

and there may be some uncertainty among rural cattle owners about the legality of shooting them.

In Botswana the law still allows farmers to shoot African wild dogs, or any other carnivore, if such an animal is considered a threat to themselves or their property.

Enforcement of the laws for the protection and management of wildlife may be both the most difficult and the single most important factor concerning wildlife in Botswana. Because of the fast-changing face of natural-resource management, wildlife laws in Botswana are continually being amended, as the government tries to accommodate current needs and pressures.

New and improved laws are useless, however, if they are not understood by the general population and enforced. Existing methods of informing the general public – through village meetings, radio programmes and word of mouth – may be too inefficient to keep up with the changes. Many people in rural areas are inadequately informed of changes in laws that directly affect them, such as laws regarding compensation, hunting or changes to boundaries of wildlife-management and protected areas.

This tendency for many rural natural-resource users to be poorly informed about the laws meant to oversee the resources puts great

Above. *A breeding herd of elephants crosses an open flood plain to return to the refuge afforded by the wooded islands. Endangered elsewhere in Africa, elephants are numerous in the lush wetlands of the Okavango.*
Right. *Caught with a flash while creeping in to have a close look at the photographer, this young dog looks sheepish and timid peering out from behind the grass blades.*

strain on enforcement officials, on the courts and on the resources, and the resulting antagonism serves to further alienate rural people from central government.

In addition to being hampered by a lack of information about changes in wildlife laws, effective enforcement is limited by several other factors. These include a lack of trained Department of Wildlife and National Parks staff and of vehicles to effectively monitor protected areas. The general distrust of government personnel and an inability to defend the boundaries of protected areas because of size and remoteness are also factors. Lastly, policies which may appear sound on paper sometimes simply do not work

in practice, due to logistical or practical constraints – the compensation policy for livestock losses that many do not take advantage of because they feel it is too slow or unfair is a good example of this.

It would seem that reasonably consistent wildlife law enforcement, such as regulating hunting licences and prohibiting cattle inside protected areas, would go a long way towards the effective management of the country's rich natural resources.

We value wild dogs because we feel they are an integral part of nature, an endangered species that needs to be protected. A local herdsman does not apply the same value, however. For

wildlife and people to benefit from the natural resources of an ecosystem, the development and management of acceptable relationships between the resources and its many users is required.

The current government of Botswana has demonstrated with legislative action that it is aware of the need for aggressive wildlife management if the wildlife of the region, including the wild dog, is to survive into the next few decades. The challenge is to understand the nature of the conflicts, develop viable solutions in which the collective values of the local communities are targeted and changed in favour of sustaining wildlife populations, and commit to implementing and enforcing these solutions for the long term.

Left. *The behavioural flexibility of wild dogs is evidenced by the 'swamp dogs' of the delta.*
Above. *The perennial swamp seems to be an endless sea of water broken only by lush green papyrus, small islands and, in the distance, a few open flood plains.*

Below. *Lechwe in flight take no chances by staying too long in the water and perhaps falling prey to an opportunistic crocodile, and seem to spend much of their escape in the air. The 'swamp dogs' take advantage of the regional abundance of antelope such as these.*

Changing Values

Historically, the Basarwa of Botswana relied on wildlife for their survival, and wildlife was the common currency that held together Botswana's various cultural, social and economic networks. As cattle began to play a greater role in Botswana's culture and value systems, however, relationships with wildlife changed.

Wildlife, once considered the property of all people, now falls under the administration and management of the somewhat intangible central government. The allocation of hunting quotas, the implementation of compensation pro-grammes, the distribution and sale of hunting

licences, and even the ownership of wildlife, are now the responsibilities of the Botswana Department of Wildlife and National Parks.

> When I was young, my father would beat me if I didn't watch the cattle. I had to stay with them all day and bring them home at night. He was proud of his cattle and proud of me. Today it is different. The younger generation are confused. They still value the cattle and want to have them, and yet they do not value the lifestyle of a cattle herder or want to be one. They want to go to the city, get a job.
>
> Everyone wants to be a big man with many cattle, so they buy cattle, but can't afford a herd boy. They just let them roam free. That is why there are so many cows on the road.
>
> *Interview, LPB, 29 June 1995.*

Ironically, however, the social common value system provided by cattle has also begun to break down in the rural areas of northern Botswana. The traditional lifestyle of rural cattle farming is in decline as the numerous attractions of hustling towns and cities draw many young people away from rural areas, but the value of cattle as representative of wealth persists.

At first, the decline of the traditional cattle farming lifestyle in Botswana would seem to be at least a step towards reducing the cultural emphasis on cattle. However, the trend actually contributes to the problem of conflict with wildlife. The reduction in the value of the traditional lifestyle leads to absentee ownership of cattle and a reduced incentive to manage cattle-ranging practices. This, in turn, leads to increased conflict with wildlife (through predation) and exaggerated environmental degradation (through overstocking). Training and education in livestock management would help encourage the proper management of existing stock, but there is little to be done about limiting the attractiveness of towns and cities to young farmers.

There is clearly an awareness of the problems associated with a growing cattle culture, such as the growing imbalance of power and wealth. Several economic developmental-aid projects have been initiated in northern Botswana. These programmes are aimed at rural communities, and

Opposite. *Left behind at the den site, a vigilant baby-sitter surveys the area to ensure no unwelcome predators happen upon the den and the unsuspecting pups.*

Above. *As the floods recede, small pools remain and make ideal watering holes and playgrounds for wild dog pups, which hesitate at the edge even though a more experienced adult is already standing in the water.*

Right. *A healthy male lion poses for a profile shot. The most social of the cats, lions live in prides and are fiercely territorial. Wild dogs regularly encounter lions in their ranges but avoid them whenever possible, even ranging in areas of lower prey density if this means a decreased chance of encountering lion.*

designed to change the focus of management by shifting some responsibility for and control of the wildlife resources back to the local communities.

Millions have been spent to change the nature of land allocation and create grassroots, community-based conservation programmes, with some areas within the Okavango region being put under the management and control of local communities. The fundamental idea is to have earnings derived from wildlife utilisation returned directly to the local communities instead of to the central government. It is hoped that once individuals begin to receive direct monetary benefit from wildlife, there will be greater incentive to invest in its long-term conservation.

Examples of community-managed wildlife which have met with success elsewhere in southern Africa include a programme of community management of wildlife in the Kaokaland in Namibia and similar projects in the Northwest Province of South Africa. These programmes

are based on the assumption that to have the incentive to manage resources responsibly, people need to have direct involvement in management decisions as well as to receive direct benefits from wildlife products and wildlife earnings. These assumptions are reasonable, and the models that are functioning elsewhere are worth pursuing.

Community-participation and resource-management projects should, however, be undertaken with care and with an in-depth knowledge of the local circumstances. Research results from efforts of this sort around the world show a remarkably high incidence of degeneration

through time. The reasons for failures, although not universal, are often related to an inability or resistance to accommodate change and the misconception that all systems are driven solely by economic incentives. As an example, a study done in the Chobe district of Botswana showed that direct monetary benefit from wildlife revenues did not significantly revise existing negative attitudes towards wildlife.

Wildlife-management policy in Botswana is based primarily on philosophies of national economic development. A concerted effort must be made to ensure that community-development

projects initiated in northern Botswana are not based only on the same assumptions. Successful wildlife-management plans cannot be developed by asking questions answerable only through quantitative or economic frameworks which do not take into account the people directly in contact with the resources at stake.

There are important – perhaps intangible – beliefs, values, cultural norms and incentives that are not always obvious and which may dictate the actions of people with respect to wildlife management, but which can be determinants in the success or failure of wildlife-management pro-

Opposite. *Seeing a normally very secretive leopard out in the open in the afternoon light is quite unusual. Of all the African carnivores, leopards have the broadest habitat and prey-species range, and will occur virtually anywhere where there is sufficient small game and enough cover to hide them.*
Left. *Nervous and jumpy, buffalo charge across bare ground, kicking up clouds of dust that can be seen for kilometres from the air.*
Below. *A young male reedbuck stands at the edge of perfect long-grass cover. Reedbuck are just the size of prey that wild dogs prefer, but their solitary habits and cryptic, nondescript coloration help them successfully evade predators.*

grammes. Understanding these is critical to the future survival of African wild dogs.

> We value cattle but they do not create employment. If we could change more cattle areas to wildlife, we could have more jobs.
> *Interview, LPB, 13 August 1995.*

The issues of sharing resources are not confined to wildlife and the local human populations. They also necessarily involve the tourism industry, the identified sustainable industry for Botswana's wildlife resources. The growing tourism market can and should effectively be tapped to aid in the conservation of threatened spaces and endangered species. A deliberate effort to educate tourists about local environmental issues of wildlife conservation and resource management could substantially modify the international emphasis on preservation in favour of sustainable utilisation. This shift alone would be a giant step towards achieving sustainable management goals. Some tour operators have already taken initiatives, providing educational tour-information packages to acquaint every tourist with local conservation issues; some of these market holidays with an

added 'conservation levy' which is given directly to local conservation programmes, emphasising that developed-world tourists to these areas can and should share with the local inhabitants in the responsibility of managing them.

The future of human growth and development is inevitable – a sobering reality. The problems associated with dwindling wild habitats are not unique to Botswana. Every country in the world faces the same problems of effectively man-aging their natural resources. It would be pleasant but impossible to preserve the Okavango and all its wildlife for all time. What we can do, however, is implement responsible management and environmental planning for the long term.

The most important aspect in any environment planning must necessarily be an accommo-dation for change – people change, needs change, the environment changes and populations grow. We can allow local communities to exercise greater control and take more responsibility for the way in which they use their natural resources. Development of the necessary infrastructure and skills may require some time, but co-management between the communities and the central govern-ment may be the best possible solution for a positive, encouraging and sustainable future for the African wild dog and wildlife in Botswana – assuming we, as a species, have the dignity to share the earth's resources with them.

Above. *A pack stalks towards an unsuspecting herd of impala in the low evening light.*
Above right. *A lone dog stands silhouetted as the last vestiges of light slowly fade away.*
Right. *An adult hovers protectively over a young pup.*

Further Reading

Social, Political and Cultural History of Botswana
Peters, Pauline E. 1994. *Dividing the Commons: Politics, Policy and Culture in Botswana*. University Press of Virginia, Charlottesville and London.
Tlou, Thomas. 1985. *A History of Ngamiland 1750-1906. The Formation of an African State*. Macmillan Botswana, Gaborone.

Wildlife, Environment, Attitudes and Conservation
Mordi, RA. 1991. *Attitudes Toward Wildlife in Botswana*. Garland Publishing Inc., New York.
Parry, D and Campbell, B. 1992. 'Attitudes of Rural Communities to Animal Wildlife and its Utilization in Chobe Enclave and Mababe Depression, Botswana' in *Environmental Conservation* Vol. 19, No. 3.
Ross, Karen. 1987. *Jewel of the Kalahari*. BBC Books, London.

Williamson, D. 1994. *Botswana, Environmental Policies and Practices under Scrutiny: The Lomba Archives*. Lindlife, Cape Town.

Wild Dogs and Other Carnivores
Bere, RM. 1956. 'The African Wild Dog' in *Orxy* 3.
Brandenburg, J. 1988. *Whitewolf: Living with an Arctic Legend*. Northwood Press, Minocqua, Wisconsin.
Childes, SL. 1988. 'The Past History, Present Status and Distribution of the Hunting Dog *Lycaon pictus* in Zimbabwe' in *Biological Conservation* 44.
Fanshawe, JH, Frame, LH and Ginsburg, J. 1991. 'The Wild Dog: Africa's Vanishing Carnivore' in *Orxy* 25 (3).
Scott, J. 1991. *Painted Wolves: Wild Dogs of the Serengeti-Mara*. Hamish Hamilton, London.

Glossary

Agropastoralism A subsistence strategy that is dependent on domesticated animals together with some seasonal cultivation.
Baby-sitter A non-parent care-giver left to attend pups at a den while the rest of the pack is away hunting.
Consorting Behavioural partnering that excludes the possibility of competitors.
Cursorial Adapted to running. A cursorial predator is one that runs down prey, as contrasted with an ambush predator.
Habituation The waning of a response due to repeated stimulation by an event that has no significant consequences, as with the gradual loss of fear of vehicles due to frequent contact with them.
Indicator Species A species that enables some overall assessment of changes in the status of a community or ecosystem.

Itinerant Temporarily present, usually to investigate or advertise, for example, for potential mating opportunities, in an area normally occupied by residents.
Nomadism A life-history characteristic of random ranging behaviour without reference to any specific geographic location.
Philopatry A life-history characteristic in which young share their natal home range with parents instead of dispersing long distances.
Resident In animal behaviour, a resident species is contrasted with a migratory species.
Ruminant A herbivore whose digestive system includes a four-chambered stomach and cud chewing to efficiently extract nutrition from plants.
Scent-marking The act of leaving substances, usually urine or faeces, that contain pheromonal (chemical) information about the scent-marker.

Index